How (Not) to Be Secular

How (Not) to Be Secular

Reading Charles Taylor

James K. A. Smith

WILLIAM B. EERDMANS PUBLISHING COMPANY
Grand Rapids, Michigan

WM. B. EERDMANS PUBLISHING CO.
2140 Oak Industrial Drive N.E., Grand Rapids, Michigan 49505
www.eerdmans.com

30 29 28 27 26 25 24 23   16 17 18 19 22 21 22 23

Library of Congress Cataloging-in-Publication Data

Smith, James K. A., 1970-
How (not) to be secular: reading Charles Taylor / James K.A. Smith.
    pages   cm
Includes bibliographical references and index.
ISBN 978-0-8028-6761-2 (pbk.: alk. paper)
1. Christian philosophy. 2. Christianity — Philosophy.
3. Taylor, Charles, 1931- Secular age. 4. Secularism.
5. Religion and culture.   I. Title.

BR100.S533   2014

230.01 — dc23

                                              2013049154

Contents

v

CONTENTS

Preface

You're a pastor or a church planter who has moved to Brooklyn or Berkeley or Boulder. Maybe you received a call to transplant yourself from Georgia or Grand Rapids or some other "religious" region of the country, sensing a burden to proclaim the gospel in one of the many so-called "godless" urban regions of North America. You've left your Jerusalem on a mission to Babylon. You came with what you thought were all the answers to the unanswered questions these "secular" people had. But it didn't take long for you to realize that the questions weren't just unanswered; they were unasked. And they weren't questions. That is, your "secular" neighbors aren't looking for "answers" — for some bit of information that is missing from their mental maps. To the contrary, they have completely different maps. You've realized that instead of nagging questions about God or the afterlife, your neighbors are oriented by all sorts of longings and "projects" and quests for significance. There doesn't seem to be anything "missing" from their lives — so you can't just come proclaiming the good news of a Jesus who fills their "God-shaped hole." They don't have any sense that the "secular" lives they've constructed are missing a second floor. In many ways, they have constructed webs of meaning that provide almost all the significance they need in their lives (though a lot hinges on that "almost").

Suffice it to say that the paradigms you brought to your ministry have failed to account for your experience thus far. You thought you were moving to a world like yours, just minus God; but in fact, you've moved to a different world entirely. It turns out this *isn't* like the Mars Hill of Saint Paul's experience (in Acts 17) where people are devoted to all kinds of deities and you get to add to their pantheon by talking about the one, true God. No, it seems that many have managed to construct a world of significance that isn't at all bothered by questions of the divine — though that world might still be *haunted* in some ways, haunted by that "almost."

Your neighbors inhabit what Charles Taylor calls an "immanent frame"; they are no longer bothered by "the God question" *as* a question because they are devotees of "exclusive humanism" — a way of being-in-the-world that offers significance without transcendence. They don't feel like anything is missing.

So what does it look like to bear witness in a secular age? What does it look like to be faithful? To what extent have Christians unwittingly absorbed the tendencies of this world? On the one hand, this raises the question of how to reach exclusive humanists. On the other hand, the question bounces back on the church: To what extent do we "believe" *like* exclusive humanists?

These are the sorts of questions this book aims to answer. Think of it as a doctor of ministry program between two covers — a philosophical ethnography of the world you inhabit, and in which you minister. Think of me as an assistant docent to this new world — coming alongside the primary guide, philosopher Charles Taylor, whose book *A Secular Age* is just the resource you didn't know you needed.

But maybe this doesn't describe you. Maybe you consider yourself "secular" — an atheist, perhaps, or at least agnostic, and generally just completely unconcerned with God or religion or church or any of that. It's not like you've "left" the faith or killed God; he never existed in the Brooklyn you call home. Indeed, in the circles you run in, matters of spirituality or transcendence just never arise. The existential world is flat. You're over it. Let's move on. Sure, we're all trying to "find" significance or "make" meaning and vaguely trying to figure out just what the hell this is all about. But c'mon: that doesn't mean we're going to entertain fairy tales.

Which is why you're constantly puzzled by all these people you read about in the *Times* or the *New Yorker* who are, like, *super* religious — who can't imagine that God doesn't exist. They seem to inhabit some other universe than your own.

Then one of your friends starts reading Mary Karr's memoirs, and even starts flirting with Catholicism. After a few months she invites you to St. Patrick's Cathedral on Christmas Eve and you're thinking this must just be a therapeutic strategy, a kind of puritanical form of self-medication. But you can't bring yourself to go along. So you stay home, alone, and before you know it, just as the bourbon is taking hold, one of those unbelievably ambiguous and nostalgic songs by The Postal Service comes on. You know, one of those songs with the sprite, light tune that lulls you into thinking it's just banal triviality, but then somehow you hear it again as if for the first time and all of a sudden you feel yourself *in* the song . . .

> *And I'm looking through the glass*
> *Where the light bends at the cracks*
> *And I'm screaming at the top of my lungs*
> *Pretending the echoes belong to someone —*
> *Someone I used to know.*

. . . and you're spooked by the longings this articulates, naming something that wells up in you from some subterranean cavern in your consciousness and you feel stupid that you're crying but you can't stop and you want to just blame it on the bourbon and the loneliness and yet there is the oddest taste of some distant joy calling to you in those tears and you're not sure what to do with any of this.

This book is for you, too.

On the one hand, this is a book about a book — a small field guide to a much larger scholarly tome.[1] It is both an homage and a portal to Charles Taylor's monumental *Secular Age,* a book that offers a genealogy of the secular and an archaeology of our angst. This is a commentary on a book that provides a commentary on postmodern culture.

On the other hand, this is also meant to be a kind of how-to manual — guidance on how (not) to live in a secular age. It is ultimately an adventure in self-understanding, a way to get our bearings in a "secular age" — whoever "we" might be: believers or skeptics, devout or doubting. Whether we're proclaiming the faith to the secularized or we're puzzled that there continue to be people of faith in this day and age, Charles Taylor has a story meant to help us locate where we are, and what's at stake. *That* existential aspect of Taylor's project is admittedly buried in a lot of history and

---

1. Think of it as Jean-François Lyotard meets Walker Percy; Foucault fused with Flannery O'Connor; Kierkegaard's *Present Age* crossed with Walter Benjamin's *Arcades Project.*

footnotes and long digressions. So I'm trying to distill and highlight this aspect of his argument precisely because I think it matters — and matters especially for those believers who are trying to not only remain faithful *in* a secular age but also bear witness to the divine *for* a secular age.

I am an unabashed and unapologetic advocate for the importance and originality of Taylor's project. I think *A Secular Age* is an insightful and incisive account of our globalized, cosmopolitan, pluralist present. Anyone who apprehends the sweep and force of Taylor's argument will get a sense that he's been reading our postmodern mail. His account of our "cross-pressured" situation — suspended between the malaise of immanence and the memory of transcendence — names and explains vague rumblings in the background of our experience for which we lack words.

I have several audiences in mind for this book, precisely because I believe *A Secular Age* incorporates several different veins of concern. I hope it will be a resource for social scientists, theologians, philosophers, and religious studies scholars grappling with issues of secularization and religion in our contemporary world.

But in fact, my primary audience is more existential. I hope this book will make Taylor's analysis accessible to a wide array of "practitioners" — by which I

This is a philosophical handbook intended for practitioners. To translate and unpack the implications of Taylor's scholarly argument for practice — especially ministry — I will employ callout boxes like this one to raise questions for reflection and to consider some of the applications and implications that *A Secular Age* raises for the practice of faith.

mean, simply, those of us living *in* this cultural moment, who feel the cross-pressures and malaise and "fragilization" that he identifies, those who have absorbed mental maps of our secular age from Death Cab for Cutie and David Foster Wallace. They might be artists or entrepreneurs, screenwriters or design consultants, baristas or political staffers — but they all intuit what Taylor is trying to diagnose: that our "secular" age is messier than many would lead us to believe; that transcendence and immanence bleed into one another; that faith is pretty much unthinkable, but abandonment to the abyss is even more so; and that they need to forge meaning and significance *in* this "secular" space rather than embracing modes of resentful escape from it. I'm thinking of my friends in Brooklyn and Berkeley, in Chicago's Wicker Park and adjacent to Manhattan's Central Park, in Toronto and Vancouver but also Milwaukee and Boulder, who have forged lives of significance that are nonetheless haunted by the ghosts of a secular age.

Among those friends are ministers, pastors, church planters, and social workers who are engaged in "religious" work in a secular age. Heirs of Dorothy Day and heralds of an almost unbelievable Story, they refuse to retreat to homogenous zones of shared plausibility structures. In fact, these are the core audience for this book precisely because I believe Taylor's analysis can help pastors and church planters understand better the contexts in which they proclaim the gospel. In many ways, Taylor's *Secular Age* amounts to a cultural anthropology for urban mission.

At the same time, Taylor's account should also serve as a wake-up call for the church, functioning as a mirror to help us see how we have come to inhabit our secular age. Taylor is not only interested in understanding how "the secular" emerged; he is also an acute observer of how we're all secular now. The secular touches everything. It not only makes *un*belief possible; it also *changes belief* — it impinges upon Christianity (and all religious communities). So Taylor's account also diagnoses the roots and extent of Christianity's assimilation — and hints at how we might cultivate resistance.

Finally, I also think Taylor offers a lexicon for cultural analysis and understanding. So I have **bolded** some of his unique terms and phrases because I think they could be introduced into our vocabularies — including the vocabularies of engaged practitioners — as a helpful shorthand. These are concisely defined in a glossary that tries to orient the reader to Taylor's technical vocabulary. The glossary might also be helpful as the reader tries to follow the thread of Taylor's argument — a quick way to reorient himself or herself while in the midst of the book.

My goal is concise commentary, identifying the thread and logic of Taylor's argument in a condensed form. You might say I'm trying to give readers a map of the forest that is *A Secular Age,* hoping to provide orientation so they can enter the larger forest of Taylor's book and thus attend to all the trees therein. In the process of concisely outlining and summarizing his argument and analysis, I have also tried to gloss some of his claims in a way that highlights their existential import, sometimes by

providing contemporary cultural hooks and examples that might resonate with younger readers. While this book could be read independently
by those unable to wade through the larger tome, ultimately my little book
is meant to be a companion to the mother ship that is Taylor's big book.
For those following along at home, this book is organized in parallel to
Taylor's outline: my five chapters correspond to the five parts of *A Secular
Age;* within those chapters, my sections roughly correspond to Taylor's
chapters.

*   *   *

The core of this book emerged from one of the highlights of my teaching
career: a 2011 senior seminar devoted to a close (and complete!) reading
of Taylor's *Secular Age.* I'm profoundly grateful to the marvelous collection of students in that class who not only waded through a long, difficult
text but also helped me to appreciate how the book touched a nerve for
them, giving them categories and language to understand their present,
including their malaise. It was their response to the book's argument that
led me to believe a book like this might help others.

I am deeply indebted to Chris Ganski and Rob Joustra, who took time
out of busy schedules to read a first draft of this manuscript. If this book
is helpful to some readers, it's due in no small part to their feedback and
suggestions.

I'm also grateful to Jon Pott and Michael Thomson, editors at Eerdmans,
for welcoming a book like this, and patiently awaiting its completion.

As usual, my writing of this book was shaped by a veritable soundtrack
— the artists who accompanied my writing in coffee shops in various
neighborhoods of Grand Rapids. In the spirit of Taylor, I gravitated toward
albums that reflected the malaise and cross-pressures and furtive wonder
that characterize our secular age. So readers might set the mood for this
book by listening to The Postal Service, Death Cab for Cutie, Fleet Foxes,
and especially Arcade Fire's unique, holistic meditation, *The Suburbs.*

Our Cross-Pressured Present: Inhabiting a Secular Age

Pascal knew that Montaigne was cheating:
to most humans, curiosity about higher things comes naturally,
it's indifference to them that must be learned.[1]

Mapping This Present Age

Imagine a map of our present — of "this present age," as Kierkegaard once put it. What's the shape of the existential terrain in which we find ourselves in late modernity? Where are the valleys of despair and mountains of bliss, the pitfalls and dead ends? What are the sites of malaise and regions of doubt? Where are the spaces of meaning? Are they hidden in secluded places, or waiting to be discovered in the mundane that is always with us? Where should we look for the "thin places" that still seem haunted by transcendence? Or have they disappeared, torn up to make way for progress and development? Where's that yawning existential abyss portrayed with clichéd abandon in *Garden State*?

---

1. Mark Lilla, "The Hidden Lesson of Montaigne," *New York Review of Books* 58, no. 5 (March 24, 2011): 20, reviewing Sarah Bakewell, *How to Live; or, A Life of Montaigne in One Question and Twenty Attempts at an Answer* (New York: The Other Press, 2011).

1

Could we imagine an existential map of our secular age that would actually help us to locate ourselves and give us a feel for where we are?

Like those hucksters on Venice Beach offering maps to the homes of the stars, there is no shortage of voices hawking road atlases for a secular age. Confident "new atheists," for example, delineate where we are with a new bravado. Employing a kind of intellectual colonialism, new atheist cartographers rename entire regions of our experience and annex them to natural science and empirical explanation, flattening the world by disenchantment. (Graveyards of the gods are always a highlight of this tour.) At the same time — and sometimes as a reaction — various fundamentalisms seem intent on selling us maps to buried treasure, pulling out yellowed parchments and trying to convince us that these dated maps tell us the truth about ourselves, about our present. But their maps are just as flat, and we feel like they're hiding something. We feel like there are whole regions of our experience they've never set foot upon — as if they claim to have mapped Manhattan because they visited Madison Square Garden. Who's going to buy *that* map?

Both of these sorts of maps are blunt instruments. They are road atlases that merely show us well-worn thoroughfares, the streets and interstates of our late modern commerce. They do nothing to map the existential wilderness of the present — those bewildering places in which we are beset by an existential vertigo. These neat and tidy color-coded road atlases are of no help when we find ourselves disoriented in a secular age, haunted by doubt or belief, by predawn fears of ghosts in the machine or a vague sense of the twilight of the idols. These road atlases of belief *versus* disbelief, religion *versus* **secularism**, belief *versus* reason provide maps that are much neater and tidier than the spaces in which we find ourselves. They give us a world of geometric precision that doesn't map onto the world of our lived experience where these matters are much fuzzier, much more intertwined — where "the secular" and "the religious" haunt each other in a mutual dance of displacement and decentering.

Rather than a ham-fisted road atlas, what we need to get our bearings is a detailed topographic map of our secular age — a relief map attuned to the uneven terrain whose contour lines help us find ourselves in the wilderness of our doubts,[2] and even the wilderness of our belief. An existen-

---

2. Note that in Mauriac's *Vipers' Tangle*, it is the materialist who is beset by doubts.

tial relief map would give us a feel for this ground that sometimes seems to be shifting beneath our feet. It would help us appreciate the complex and complicated terrain of our secular age, the curve of our earthbound longings. By representing depth and height, ascent and descent, an existential relief map has room to acknowledge those hauntings of transcendence that sometimes sneak up on us in our otherwise mundane disenchantment. At the same time, such a contoured existential cartograph should also help us feel the suffocating immanence that characterizes late modern existence, even for "believers."

Charles Taylor's *Secular Age* is that kind of book.[3] You might not guess it, glancing at the intimidating 900-page tome on the shelf. Buried in the long historical narrative and philosophical analysis is an existential map of our present — an argument that should find a home in cafés and living rooms, not just in lecture halls and seminar rooms. At its heart, *A Secular Age* is charting terrain mapped by the likes of Camus and Death Cab for Cutie more than staid social scientists and philosophers. Indeed, there is something fundamentally literary, even poetic, in Taylor's prosaic account of our "secular age" — this pluralized, pressurized moment in which we find ourselves, where believers are beset by doubt and doubters, every once in a while, find themselves tempted by belief.[4] It is Taylor's complexity, nuance, and refusal of simplistic reductionisms that make him a reliable cartographer who provides genuine orientation in our secular age. *A Secular Age* is the map of globalized Gotham, a philosophical ethnography of our present.

Haunting Immanence

Taylor names and identifies what some of our best novelists, poets, and artists attest to: that our age is haunted. On the one hand, we live under a brass heaven, ensconced in immanence. We live in the twilight of both

---

3. Charles Taylor, *A Secular Age* (Cambridge: Harvard University Press, Belknap Press, 2007). Page references to this work will be placed directly in the text; the title of the work *(Secular Age)* will occasionally preface the page reference when confusion with other Taylor works is possible.

4. We will return to the centrality of "story" in Taylor's project below.

gods and idols. But their ghosts have refused to depart, and every once in a while we might be surprised to find ourselves tempted by belief, by intimations of transcendence. Even what Taylor calls the **"immanent frame"** is haunted. On the other hand, even as faith endures in our secular age, believing doesn't come easy. Faith is fraught; confession is haunted by an inescapable sense of its contestability. We don't believe instead of doubting; we believe *while* doubting. We're all Thomas now.

The wager of this book — like the gambit of Taylor's *Secular Age* — is that most of us live in this cross-pressured space, where both our agnosticism and our devotion are mutually haunted and haunting. If our only guides were new atheists or religious fundamentalists, we would never know that this vast, contested terrain even existed, even though most of us live in this space every day. But if we put away the flattened fundamentalist atlases and pick up a detailed existential relief map like *A Secular Age,* we find a guide that is attuned to the reverberations of our haunted immanent frame. Such a guide "makes sense" of our situation not by didactically explaining it, and certainly not by explaining it *away,* but by giving us the words to name what we've *felt.*

This is why Taylor's close partners in such a task tend to be novelists. Consider, for example, Julian Barnes's *Nothing to Be Frightened Of* as an example of another existential map of our secular age. The book is penned as a response to what he calls, cribbing from French critic Charles du Bos, *le réveil mortel.* On Barnes's account, a first, clunky translation of the phrase remains the best. Though " 'the wake-up call to mortality' sounds a bit like a hotel service," in fact this translation's metaphor hits just the right note: "it *is* like being in an unfamiliar hotel room, where the alarm clock has been left on the previous occupant's setting, and at some ungodly hour you are suddenly pitched from sleep into darkness, panic, and a vicious awareness that this is a rented world."[5] It is just this sort of unanticipated wake-up call that many experience, even in a "secular" age.

Nothing to Be Frightened Of is Barnes's way of grappling with this wake-up call to mortality, which seems to have jarred him from his slumbers at a young age and has been harassing him ever since, as if he's been

---

5. Julian Barnes, *Nothing to Be Frightened Of* (London: Jonathan Cape, 2008), p. 23. In-text page references in the next few paragraphs are to Barnes's book.

unable to change the settings on that hotel room clock. But he receives this as a challenge to find the words to, if not make sense of, at least be articulate about *le réveil mortel* — a veritable gauntlet that death throws down at the writer's feet. At one point he castigates himself for failing in the face of this challenge:

> Only a couple of nights ago, there came again that alarmed and alarming moment, of being pitch-forked back into consciousness, awake, alone, utterly alone, beating pillow with fist shouting "oh no Oh No OH NO" in an endless wail, the horror of the moment — the minutes — overwhelming what might, to an objective witness, appear a shocking display of self-exhibitionist pity. An inarticulate one, too: for what sometimes shames me is the extraordinary lack of descriptive, or responsive, words that come out of my mouth. For God's sake, you're a *writer,* I say to myself. You do *words.* Can't you improve on that? Can't you face down death — well, you won't ever face it down, but can't you at least protest against it — more interestingly than this? (p. 126)

Barnes himself has suggested that it was Flaubert who found a language for sex; Edmund Wilson claimed that D. H. Lawrence finally found an English vocabulary for the same. We might suggest that Barnes has written a book that picks up the gauntlet, hoping to find a language for death. In his hands, the language of death is democratic — which makes good sense since death is quite impartial (talk about *e pluribus unum!*). And, as one would expect from Barnes, the language of death also turns out to be funny as hell. But it is a lexicon that is always haunted, one that can never quite shake the ghosts of transcendence.

"I don't believe in God, but I miss Him." This is the opening line of the book, described by the author's philosopher-brother as "soppy." Despite being solidly secular in a way that must still seem exotic to many Americans outside the cordoned spaces of Manhattan or Seattle ("I was never baptized, never sent to Sunday school. I have never been to a normal church service in my life" [p. 15]), Barnes does not offer merely secularized meditations on death. Questions in the orbit of death and extinction inevitably raise questions about eternity and afterlife, till pretty soon you find yourself bumping up against questions about God and divinity.

Barnes follows the questions where they might lead, and shows an understanding of some of the nuances of Christianity that are missed by others in his generation.

That's not to say he isn't up front about his agnosticism. As part of an inverse hagiography, Barnes shows an interest in conversions to atheism and agnosticism, querying his family and friends regarding when and how they lost their faith (not unlike new evangelical friends who are interested in when I became a Christian — by which they mean, *date* and *time,* please). Barnes's own testimony in this regard is entirely adolescent and completely honest: "My own final letting go of the remnant, or possibility, of religion, happened at a later age. As an adolescent, hunched over some book or magazine in the family bathroom, I used to tell myself that God couldn't possibly exist because the notion that He might be watching me while I masturbated was absurd; even more absurd was the notion that all my dead ancestors might be lined up and watching too. . . . The thought of Grandma and Grandpa observing what I was up to would have seriously put me off my stroke" (p. 16). No evidential problem of evil; no intellectual dissatisfaction with the doctrine of the incarnation; no vaulted claims to rational enlightenment; just an honest, onanistic confession of a rather pragmatic agnosticism. But more titillating, in fact, is Barnes's mature reflection on this loss of faith:

> In her much-discussed book *When God Talks Back,* anthropologist Tanya Luhrmann asks: "If you could believe in God, why wouldn't you?" At the same time, she concedes: "It ought to be difficult to believe in God." To live in a secular age is to inhabit just this space and tension. **What are the implications of this for Christian witness in a secular age? How do we recognize and affirm the *difficulty* of belief?**

> As I record this now, however, I wonder why I didn't think through more of the possibilities. Why did I assume that God, if He *was* watching, necessarily disapproved of how I was spilling my seed? Why did it not occur to me that if the sky did not fall in as it witnessed my zealous and unflagging self-abuse, this might be because the sky did not judge it a sin? Nor did I have the imagination to conceive of my dead ancestors equally smiling on my actions: go on, my son, enjoy it while you've got it, there won't be

much more of that once you're a disembodied spirit, so have another one
for us. (p. 16)

He thus owns up to his "breezy illogic" in moments of self-critique, and the
critique of others who lost faith in God because of unanswered prayers: "No
subsequent reflection from any of us that perhaps God's main business,
were He to exist, might not be as an adolescent helpline, goods-provider,
or masturbation-scourge. No, out with Him once and for all" (pp. 45-46).

Unlike so many secularist writers who are happy to caricature religion
whenever possible, Barnes resists such easy targets. But he also resists
de-fanging religion. Indeed, the agnostic Barnes can sometimes be a surprising apologist for what might be construed as "conservative" religion.
Intolerant of squishy spirituality, he finds "the notion of redefining the
deity into something that works for you" nothing short of "grotesque"
(p. 46). At a dinner party with neighbors he overheard a young man shout
sarcastically, "But why should God do that for His son and not for the
rest of us?" "Because He's *God*, for Christ's sake" (p. 77), Barnes shouted
back. Taking up the mantle of agnostic prophet, he hurls criticism at
the idolatries of "C of E" niceties, in a way that surprisingly echoes Cardinal Newman's famous critique of "Liberalism": "there seems little
point," Barnes muses, "in a religion which is merely a weekly social event
(apart, of course, from the normal pleasures of a weekly social event), as
opposed to one which tells you exactly how to live, which colours and
stains everything" (p. 64). The metaphor returns later: "What's the point
of faith unless you and it are serious — *seriously* serious — unless your
religion fills, directs, stains and sustains your life?" (p. 81). If the young
Barnes thought a God who cared about stains on his trousers couldn't
possibly exist, the older Barnes thinks the only religion worth embracing
(and rejecting) is one that stains everything.

It's hard not to read *Nothing to Be Frightened Of* against the backdrop
of "new atheist" best sellers by Dawkins, Dennett, Harris, and Hitchens.
But Julian Barnes will not be anthologized in the next edition of *The Porta-
ble Atheist*. Unlike Ian McEwan and Salman Rushdie (literary figures with
their own epistles in Hitchens's canon), Barnes lacks the fundamentalist
swagger of the new atheists. In particular, he lacks their chronological
snobbery and their epistemological confidence:

If I called myself an atheist at twenty, and an agnostic at fifty and sixty, it isn't because I've acquired more knowledge in the meantime: just more awareness of ignorance. How can we be sure that we know enough to know? As twenty-first century neo-Darwinian materialists, convinced that the meaning and mechanism of life have only been fully clear since the year 1859, we hold ourselves categorically wiser than those credulous knee-benders who, a speck of time away, believed in divine purpose, an ordered world, resurrection and a Last Judgment. But although we are more informed, we are no more evolved, and certainly no more intelligent than them. What convinces us our knowledge is so final? (pp. 23-24)

Given his own epistemological tentativeness, Barnes can't resist a bit of fun, imagining a divine game at the expense of our celebrity atheists:

If there were a games-playing God, He would surely get especial ludic pleasure from disappointing those philosophers who had convinced themselves and others of His non-existence. A. J. Ayer assures Somerset Maugham that there is nothing, and nothingness, after death: whereupon they both find themselves players in God's little end-of-the-pier entertainment called Watch the Fury of the Resurrected Atheist. That's a neat would-you-rather for the God-denying philosopher: would you rather there was nothing after death, and you were proved right, or that there was a wonderful surprise, and your professional reputation was destroyed? (p. 208)

In short, Barnes has nothing to do with the silliness that claims that "religion poisons everything."

Not surprisingly, where Barnes really appreciates the haunting of immanence is in the realm of the aesthetic.[6] Barnes's appreciation for religious art — both painting and music — is one of the best aspects of the book, and leaves him a little spooked. "Missing God is focused for me," he confesses, "by missing the underlying sense of purpose and belief when confronted with religious art" (p. 54). He seems, if not tempted by, at least a bit intrigued by an *aesthetic* argument never

---

6. I say "not surprisingly" since, as we'll see below, Taylor also highlights art as a particularly important site of "cross-pressure" in a secular age. See *Secular Age,* pp. 605-9.

entertained in Aquinas's "Five Ways": that religion might just be true simply because it is beautiful. "The Christian religion didn't last so long merely because everyone believed it" (p. 53), Barnes observes. It lasted because it makes for a helluva novel — which is pretty close to Tolkien's claim that the gospel is true because it is the most fantastic fantasy, the greatest fairy story ever told.[7] And Barnes, a great lover of both music and painting, knows that much of what he enjoys owes its existence to Christianity. Without the madness of the gospel, Mozart would never have composed a requiem, Giotto would never have left us the treasures in the chapel of Padua. Thus he finds himself asking, "What if it were true?" — a question never entertained by the dogmaticians of the new atheism. What would it be like, he asks, to listen to Mozart's *Requiem* and take it as nonfiction?[8]

In this openness to haunting, Barnes remains a good disciple of Flaubert, of whom he comments: "While he distrusted religions, he had a tenderness towards the spiritual impulse, and was suspicious of militant atheism. 'Each dogma in itself is repulsive to me,' he wrote. 'But I consider the feeling that engendered them to be the most natural and poetic expression of humanity. I don't like those philosophers who have dismissed it as foolishness and humbug. What I find there is necessity and instinct. So I respect the black man kissing his fetish as much as I do the Catholic kneeling before the Sacred Heart' " (p. 172). It is Barnes's Flaubertian self-suspicion that is both interesting and winsome — not because it provides comfort or fodder for faith, but because it illustrates the possibility of being an atheist without being a fundamentalist. The doubter's doubt is faith; his temptation is be-

---

7. See J. R. R. Tolkien, "On Fairy-Stories," in *Tree and Leaf* (London: HarperCollins, 2001), pp. 3-80.

8. Unfortunately, at this point Barnes constructs a false dichotomy: "The Christian," he surmises, "would . . . have been concerned more with truth than aesthetics." Whence the distinction? One might say that the madness of the incarnation obliterates such a dichotomy, that the logic of incarnation scandalously claims that truth and beauty kiss (cp. Ps. 85:10). Taking it to be true does not trump the beauty; receiving it as nonfiction does not de-aestheticize the work of art, reducing it to a textbook. But though Barnes's dichotomy is misplaced, it seems laudable that he entertains what it would mean for these works of art to also be *more* than (merely) aesthetic. "It is one of the haunting hypotheticals for the non-believer," he concludes: "what would it be like 'if it were true' " (p. 54).

lief, and it is a temptation that has not been entirely quelled, even in a secular age.[9]

Doubting Transcendence

But the haunting is mutual, which is why religious literature in our secular age attests to the persistent specter of doubt. Outside of Amish fiction and Disney-fied versions of biblical narratives, believers in contemporary literature are "**fragilized**," as Taylor will describe it. While Flannery O'Connor was an ethnographer of the "Christ-haunted" South, that world was just as haunted by the Antichrist. As Paul Elie aptly notes, twentieth-century fiction was where we saw that "the churchgoer was giving way to the moviegoer."[10]

What Taylor describes as "secular" — a situation of fundamental contestability when it comes to belief, a sense that rival stories are always at the door offering a very different account of the world — is the engine that drove Flannery O'Connor's fiction. As she attested in a letter about her first novel:

> I don't think you should write something as long as a novel around anything that is not of the gravest concern to you and everybody else, and for me this is always the conflict between an attraction for the Holy and the disbelief in it that we breathe in with the air of our times. It's hard to believe always but more so in the world we live in now. There are some of us who have to pay for our faith every step of the way and who have to work

9. This is pictured in François Mauriac's classic, *Vipers' Tangle,* trans. Warren B. Wells (New York: Image/Doubleday, 1957). In a Christopher Hitchens–like preemptive note, the curmudgeonly, miserly Louis warns his family that should he, upon his deathbed, call a priest, they should merely chalk this up to irrational weakness. But he later makes a confession: "it is, on the contrary, when I study myself, as I have been doing for the past two months, with a curiosity which is stronger than my disgust; it is when I feel myself most fully in possession of my faculties that the Christian temptation torments me. I can no longer deny that a route exists in me which might lead me to your God" (p. 104).

10. Paul Elie, *The Life You Save May Be Your Own: An American Pilgrimage* (New York: Farrar, Straus and Giroux, 2003), p. 320 — alluding, of course, to Walker Percy, *The Moviegoer* (New York: Vintage, 1998 [1961]).

out dramatically what it would be like without it and if being without it would be ultimately possible or not.[11]

Even a faith that wants to testify and evangelize — as certainly O'Connor did — has to do so *from* this place. Indeed, consider the *dramatis personae* of religiously attuned literature over the past fifty years, from Graham Greene's whisky priest to Walker Percy's Dr. Thomas More to Evelyn Waugh's Charles Ryder, even Marilynne Robinson's Protestant pastor in *Gilead:* not a one matches the caricature of either the new atheists' straw men or fundamentalist confidence. Their worlds seem as fraught as our own — and *more* honestly fraught than the areligious, de-transcendentalized universes created by Ian McEwan or Jonathan Franzen.

Elie, whose fourfold biography is an encapsulation of the fate of faith in a secular age, well summarizes the effect:

> We are all skeptics now, believer and unbeliever alike. There is no one true faith, evident at all times and places. Every religion is one among many. The clear lines of any orthodoxy are made crooked by our experience, are complicated by our lives. Believer and unbeliever are in the same predicament, thrown back onto themselves in complex circumstances, looking for a sign. As ever, religious belief makes its claim somewhere between revelation and projection, between holiness and human frailty; but the burden of proof, indeed the burden of belief, for so long upheld by society, is now back on the believer, where it belongs.[12]

While Taylor will complicate that last flourish of individualism, the diagnosis and description are the same: there's no going back. Ardor and devotion cannot undo the shift in plausibility structures that characterizes our age. There's no undoing the secular; there's just the task of learning how (not) to live — and perhaps even believe — in a secular age.

It might be hard for the nonreligious to imagine that some believers

---

11. Cited in Elie, *The Life You Save,* p. 155. In another context, Walker Percy once recounted: "When it is asked just so, straight out, just so: 'Why are you a Catholic?' I usually reply, 'What else is there?'" ("Why Are You a Catholic?" in Walker Percy, *Signposts in a Strange Land,* ed. Patrick Samway [New York: Picador, 1991], p. 307).

12. Elie, *The Life You Save,* p. 427.

welcome this situation. Walker Percy, for example, welcomed the disestablishment of Christendom. Writing to his lifelong friend Shelby Foote, Percy mused that "Christendom no longer can or even should call the tune. If Christians believe in the kingdom, that's their business, but they should realize that the world has by and large turned away. There is no longer such a thing as Christendom, and as Kierkegaard said, maybe it's just as well."[13] Twenty years later he would repeat the same theme, effectively praising "the secular" as described by Taylor: "the present age," he surmised, "is better than Christendom. In the old Christendom, everyone was a Christian and hardly anyone thought twice about it. But in the present age the survivor of theory and consumption becomes a wayfarer in the desert, like St. Anthony; which is to say, open to signs."[14] This is a Catholic embrace of "secularity" as Taylor defines it, demonstrating that the terrain can't be neatly carved up into rational secularists and resentful believers.

Indeed, on Taylor's account, ardent secular*ism* has not appreciated or embraced secular*ity*. And he thinks that, in some fleeting moments of aesthetic enchantment or mundane haunting, even the secularist is pressed by a sense of something more — some **"fullness"** that wells up within (or presses down upon) the managed immanent frame we've constructed in modernity. In the same way, postmodern believers can't shield themselves from competing stories that call into question the fundamental Story of faith. Evolutionary psychology and **expressive individualism** are in the water of our secular age, and only a heroic few can manage to quell their chatter to create an insulated panic room in which their faith remains solidly secure.[15]

Ours is a "secular" age, according to Taylor, not because of any index of religious participation (or lack thereof), but because of these sorts of manifestations of contested meaning. It's as if the cathedrals are still standing, but their footings have been eroded. Conversely, the Nietz-

13. Letter of February 3, 1971, in *The Correspondence of Shelby Foote and Walker Percy*, ed. Jay Tolson (New York: Norton, 1997), p. 154.

14. Percy, "Why Are You a Catholic?" p. 314.

15. Actually, what often happens in these cases is some fundamental accession to some aspect of a competing narrative — for example, the individualism of the American republic — which is then assimilated to a mutated version of faith.

schean dream is alive and well, and the heirs of Bertrand Russell and Auguste Comte continue to beat their drums, and yet Oprah and Elizabeth Gilbert still make it to the best seller lists and the magic of Tolkien still captivates wide audiences. Even a late modern hero like Steve Jobs doesn't conform to the narrative of secularism. In his biography of Jobs, Walter Isaacson recalls a scene near the end of Jobs's life that exemplifies the ambiguity of our secular age:

> One sunny afternoon, when he wasn't feeling well, Jobs sat in the garden behind his house and reflected on death. He talked about his experiences in India almost four decades earlier, his study of Buddhism, and his views on reincarnation and spiritual transcendence. "I'm about fifty-fifty on believing in God," he said. "For most of my life, I've felt that there must be more to our existence than meets the eye."
>
> He admitted that, as he faced death, he might be overestimating the odds out of a desire to believe in an afterlife. "I like to think that something survives after you die," he said. "It's strange to think that you accumulate all this experience, and maybe a little wisdom, and it just goes away. So I really want to believe that something survives, that maybe your consciousness endures."
>
> He fell silent for a very long time. "But on the other hand, perhaps it's like an on-off switch," he said. "*Click!* And you're gone."
>
> Then he paused again and smiled slightly. "Maybe that's why I never liked to put on-off switches on Apple devices."[16]

In such contexts, Taylor is apt to quote Peggy Lee: "Is that all there is?" One could update the lyrical reference a bit with almost anything coming out of Seattle in the 1990s. Consider, for example, The Postal Service's curious lament in "Clark Gable":

> *I want so badly to believe*
> *that there is truth, that love is real.*
> *And I want life in every word,*
> *to the extent that it's absurd.*

16. Walter Isaacson, *Steve Jobs* (New York: Simon and Schuster, 2011), pp. 570-71.

Or I can recall the conclusion of a Radiohead concert in Alpine Valley, Wisconsin, feeling the tensions and contradictions as Thom Yorke eerily crooned, "Everything In Its Right Place" while "FOREVER" constantly looped on a screen behind the band and the music itself generated a sense of longing and transcendence that clearly captivated the entire audience. These are the sorts of postmodern phenomena that Taylor helps us make sense of. While stark fundamentalisms — either religious or secular — get all the press, what should interest us are these fugitive expressions of doubt *and* longing, faith *and* questioning. These lived expressions of **"cross-pressure"** are at the heart of the secular.

David Foster Wallace might be a shining example of such fugitive configurations of meaning in postmodernity.[17] Wallace's corpus — both fiction and nonfiction — documents a world of almost suffocating immanence, a flattened human universe where the escapes are boredom and distraction, not ecstasy and rapture.[18] Hell is self-consciousness, and our late modern, TV-ized (now Twitter-ized) world only ramps up our self-awareness to an almost paralyzing degree. God is dead, but he's replaced by everybody else. Everything is permitted, but everybody is watching. So most of the time the best "salvation" we can hope for is found in behaviors that numb us to this reality: drugs, sex, entertainments of various sorts.

And yet. Contrary to the picture sketched by Dreyfus and Kelly, there is a persistent hint that David Foster Wallace is spooked; that his world is haunted. His characters are anything but satisfied with what late modern capitalism has to offer, and so we see regular glimpses of what Taylor calls the **"nova effect"** — new modes of being that try to forge a way through,

17. What follows is, I hope, a not-so-oblique response to what I take to be the gross misreading of Wallace offered by Hubert Dreyfus and Sean Dorrance Kelly in *All Things Shining: Reading the Western Classics to Find Meaning in a Secular Age* (New York: Free Press, 2011), pp. 22-57. *All Things Shining* is its own not-so-oblique response to Taylor's *Secular Age*. As the authors frame it, "Our view is that nihilism is every bit as closed-minded as fanaticism, and that neither is a sufficient ground on which to base a livable life. But we are more skeptical than Taylor that Judeo-Christian monotheism can be culturally satisfying in the modern age" (p. 21).

18. However, Dreyfus and Kelly are factually wrong when they claim that "God casts no shadow at all in the world of *Infinite Jest*" (*All Things Shining*, p. 45). See my discussion of the role of religion and invocations of God in Wallace's book *Infinite Jest* in James K. A. Smith, *Imagining the Kingdom: How Worship Works* (Grand Rapids: Baker Academic, 2013), chap. 1.

even out of, the cross-pressured situation where immanence seems ready to implode upon itself. Take, for example, the narrator of "Good Old Neon," a stream-of-consciousness testimony allegedly generated in the flash before his suicide. This character[19] is prototypically DFW-ish insofar as he is almost possessed by self-consciousness, doomed to self-awareness, beset by a sort of secularized guilt about being fraudulent — the fraudulence arising from the root of being unable to love — and who now, in the nanoseconds before his self-inflicted death, is reflecting on how this self-consciousness "basically ruined all the best parts of everything."[20]

Only in certain insulated regions of secularism would it be so unthinkable that he might look for liberation — and a kind of exorcism — in religion. But this is not unthinkable to Wallace. Instead, we learn that this character did just that in his "holy roller phase," spending time at a charismatic church in Naperville, Illinois, "to try to wake up spiritually instead of living in this fog of fraudulence."[21] He sees and praises the beauty of the devout, and *wants* to believe, but the ghosts of self-awareness won't let him go (they are Legion), "the real truth here being how quickly I went from being someone who was there because he wanted to wake up and stop being a fraud to being somebody who was so anxious to impress the congregation with how devoted and active I was."[22] The brush with transcendence is not an escape, and certainly not a solution, but neither is it unthinkable. It's no solution to rule out transcendence either.

The hints of this become almost shouts in a posthumously published story, "All That." In it, a precocious young boy is fascinated by the fictive "magic" of a toy cement truck — a magic concocted merely by his parents saying so. In a Santa Claus–like fib, the parents tell the boy that the

---

19. There is always a temptation to read Wallace's depressives and suicides as autobiographical creations. I think it's important to not be led into that temptation, and don't assume it here. Wallace especially tries to guard against it in this story by having another character named David Wallace later read about the suicide.

20. David Foster Wallace, "Good Old Neon," in *Oblivion: Stories* (Boston: Little, Brown, 2004), p. 156. On the link between fraudulence and "a basic inability to really love," see pp. 165-66.

21. Wallace, "Good Old Neon," p. 156.

22. Wallace, "Good Old Neon," p. 157.

cement truck's mixer moves, but only when he's not looking. Impossible to confirm (since seeing it would stop it), the grown-up narrator looking back on this episode identifies the longing: "As an adult, I realize that the reason I spent so much time trying to 'catch' the drum rotating was that I wanted to verify that I could not. IF I had ever been successful in outsmarting the magic, I would have been crushed."[23] One would expect then a story of rational maturation, of putting away childish things like magic, growing up and learning to no longer be duped.[24] Wake up and smell the disenchantment.

But that's not what Wallace does.[25] To the contrary, the grown narrator, looking at his younger self, sees in this episode "the origin of the religious feeling that has informed most of my adult life" — a fundamental attitude of "reverence."[26] What passes for "atheism," he observes, is still a mode of worship, "a kind of anti-religious religion, which worships reason, skepticism, intellect, empirical proof, human autonomy, and self-determination." But the narrator is not ready to convert to the gospel of immanence. To the contrary, "the fact that the most powerful and significant connections in our lives are (at the time) invisible to us seems to me a compelling argument for religious reverence rather than skeptical empiricism as a response to life's meaning."[27] This too is haunted: by the sense that we're just making this up, that the religious is as fictive as his parents' attribution of magic to the cement mixer, that we can't trust our impulses or memories or inclinations to reverence. And yet this religious ghost can't be exorcised either.[28]

---

23. David Foster Wallace, "All That," *New Yorker,* December 14, 2009, pp. 77-81, at p. 77.

24. As we'll see below, "maturation" narratives are endemic to a certain version of secularism.

25. Again, my argument here does not depend on autobiographizing the story. I simply need to show that the world of Wallace's fiction (a world of his making) and the characters therein are characterized by a cross-pressured openness to "fullness" in ways that Dreyfus and Kelly do not appreciate. And unlike the sorts of portrayals one gets from, say, Jonathan Franzen, Wallace doesn't create such characters in order to disdain them. In other words, he doesn't portray characters as open to transcendence so that we, the readers, can congratulate ourselves on *not* being such.

26. Wallace, "All That," p. 78.

27. Wallace, "All That," p. 79.

28. In other words, Dreyfus and Kelly couldn't be more wrong about Wallace. But don't

It is my sense that more of us live in worlds like those portrayed by David Foster Wallace than those mapped by either new atheists or religious fundamentalists. It is this sort of contested, cross-pressured, haunted world that is "secular" — not a world sanitized of faith and transcendence, flattened to the empirical.

How (Not) to Be Secular

So where are we? How did we get here? And *how* does that "back story" make a difference for how we might move forward — for how we might *live* in a secular age?

To really do justice to the messy complexity of our secular age, we need

---

take my word for it: consider the testimony of Zadie Smith in *"Brief Interviews with Hideous Men:* The Difficult Gifts of David Foster Wallace," in *Changing My Mind: Occasional Essays* (London: Hamish Hamilton/Penguin, 2009), pp. 257-300, and her remarks at the memorial service for Wallace at NYU, October 23, 2008, published in *Harper's* 318, no. 1904 (January 2009): 26-29. In fact, in "Difficult Gifts," Smith sees in Wallace an interest in the "porosity" of existence — a notion that will take on new significance in the exposition of Taylor below. Because of this, she concludes, Wallace's characters "expressed a longing for the infinite" that generates "those quasi-mystical moments" in Wallace's corpus. "We might feel more comfortable calling this 'meditation,' but I believe the right word is in fact *prayer*" (pp. 297-98).

Dreyfus and Kelly will protest that their critique of Wallace is more radical: not that there aren't moments of meaning and significance, but that for Wallace, meaning and significance are only things *we* give to the world — not gifts to be received. As they put it, "the sacred in Wallace — insofar as he can see such a phenomenon at all — is something *we impose* upon experience; there is nothing *given* about it at all" (*All Things Shining*, p. 47, emphasis in original). But here again Smith offers an antithetical reading. Wallace, she observes, was deeply indebted to Lewis Hyde's cultural anthropology of the gift — not to mention the fact that he had to labor under the constant shadow of being one of the outrageously "gifted" authors of his generation, a burden you sense he would sometimes like to remit. Wallace's critique of narcissism hinges on just this point: "The narcissist feels his gifts come from himself." So, contrary to Dreyfus and Kelly's misreading, in fact Wallace valorized a stance of fundamental receptivity: "To Wallace," Smith concludes, "a gift truly was an accident, a chance, a fortuitous circumstance. Born intelligent, born with perfect pitch, with mathematical ability, with a talent for tennis — in what sense are we ever proprietors of these blessings? What rights accrue to us because of them? How could we ever truly own them?" (Smith, p. 293). Cp. 1 Cor. 4:7: "What do you have that you did not receive?"

something like "time-lapse" maps that not only provide snapshots of the current existential terrain but also give us a sense of how it got to be this way. This would be an incredible sort of map, of course: simultaneously a work of cartography and archaeology, giving us both the lay of the land and a peek at the strata beneath our feet. My goal in this book is to show that Charles Taylor's *Secular Age* is just this sort of 3-D, time-lapsed, existential map of our present, a guide we need to make sense of our age. And I hope this book will be a guide to the guide — a brief, crisp overview that will serve as an invitation to unfold the larger, more detailed map. To open up a substantive exposition of his argument and analysis, let's unpack three orienting themes that guide Taylor's project.

Taylor's Question

Our goal in trying to understand our "secular age" is not a descriptive *what*, and even less a chronological *when*, but rather an analytic *how*. The question is *not* whether our age is less (or more) "religious"; nor is it a question of trying to determine when some switch was tripped so that, in the world-historical language of Will Durant & Co., we went from an "age of belief" to an "age of reason." Instead, Taylor is concerned with the "conditions of belief" — a shift in the plausibility conditions that make something believable or unbelievable.[29] So *A Secular Age* is persistently asking and reasking various permutations of the following questions:

> "How did we move from a condition where, in Christendom, people lived naïvely within a theistic construal, to one in which we all shunt between two stances, in which everyone's construal shows up as such; and in which

---

29. It is important to appreciate that, philosophically, Taylor is working from the tradition of hermeneutic phenomenology, an heir of Heidegger and Merleau-Ponty. So he equates the "conditions" of belief with the "background" we bring to our perception of reality (*Secular Age*, p. 13). For examples of Taylor's work in epistemology that unpack the philosophical assumptions behind his methodology, see Charles Taylor, "Overcoming Epistemology," in *Philosophical Arguments* (Cambridge: Harvard University Press, 1995), pp. 1-19, and Taylor, "Merleau-Ponty and the Epistemological Picture," in *The Cambridge Companion to Merleau-Ponty*, ed. Taylor Carman and Mark B. N. Hansen (Cambridge: Cambridge University Press, 2005), pp. 26-49.

moreover, unbelief has become for many the major default option?"[30] (p. 14)

"Why was it virtually impossible not to believe in God in, say, 1500 in our Western society, while in 2000 many of us[31] find this not only easy, but even inescapable?" (p. 25)

As you'll notice, these questions are not concerned with *what* people believe as much as with what is believ*able*. The difference between our modern, "secular" age and past ages is not necessarily the catalogue of available beliefs but rather the default assumptions about what is believable. It is this way of framing the question that leads to Taylor's unique definition of "the secular."

30. Some readers stumble on Taylor's claim here because they are surrounded by communities where theism is not only quite believable, it remains the "default" for many. Reading Taylor in such locations makes it difficult to entertain his assumption here. It is important to realize that Taylor is thinking of those environs of the West where unbelief is the rule — either geographically (a number of European nations) or in terms of class. On the latter, consider Peter Berger's account of a globalized secular elite in "The Desecularization of the World: A Global Overview," in *The Desecularization of the World: Resurgent Religion and World Politics,* ed. Berger (Grand Rapids: Eerdmans, 1999), p. 10. As Berger puts it, "There exists an international subculture composed of people with Western-type higher education, especially in the humanities and social sciences, that is indeed secularized. This subculture is the principal 'carrier' of progressive, Enlightened beliefs and values. While its members are relatively thin on the ground, they are very influential, as they control the institutions that provide the 'official' definitions of reality, notably the educational system, the media of mass communication, and the higher reaches of the legal system."

31. Always be wary of first-person plurals. Who is "us"? Others have pressed Taylor for a certain parochialism that characterizes his account. As Warner, VanAntwerpen, and Calhoun frame it, "The process by which Latin Christendom got to be secular was in large part the same as the process by which it got to be colonial. Thus it is analytically inadequate to frame the 'internal' history of Latin Christendom as though this process were not internal to it. And it leaves the book oddly disengaged with the postcolonial conditions that have generated so much of the blowback against the secular." See "Editors' Introduction," in *Varieties of Secularism in a Secular Age,* ed. Michael Warner, Jonathan VanAntwerpen, and Craig Calhoun (Cambridge: Harvard University Press, 2010), p. 27. See also the chapters in this volume by José Casanova and Saba Mahmood. Taylor accepts the point in "Afterword: Apologia pro Libro suo," p. 301.

Taylor's Taxonomy of the Secular

So what does "secular" mean? What would it mean to call this a "secular" age? Taylor's question puts him on the terrain of "secularization theory" — a long-held thesis that hypothesized that religious belief would decrease as modernity progressed. Such prognostication has not proven to be true, so most debates about secularization have been wrangling about empirical data regarding rates of religious belief, etc.

Taylor is not playing that game because he thinks it's misguided and misses the point. Such debates are still focused on beliefs, whereas Taylor thinks the essence of "the secular" is a matter of believability. Secularization theorists (and their opponents) are barking up the wrong tree precisely because they fixate on *expressions* of belief rather than *conditions* of belief. Similarly, secular*ists,* who demand the decontamination of the public sphere as an areligious zone, tend to be a bit unreflective about the epistemic questions that attend their own beliefs.[32] So battles over "the secular" are usually flummoxed by the equivocal nature of the terms. Let's clarify and nuance our analysis by adopting Taylor's threefold taxonomy of "secular."

1. In classical or medieval accounts, the "secular" amounted to something like "the temporal" — the realm of "earthly"[33] politics or of "mundane" vocations. This is the "secular" of the purported sacred/secular divide. The priest, for instance, pursues a "sacred" vocation, while the butcher, baker, and candlestick maker are engaged in "sec-

32. I have pressed this point in more detail in James K. A. Smith, "Secular Liturgies and the Prospects for a 'Post-Secular' Sociology of Religion," in *The Post-Secular in Question,* ed. Philip Gorski et al. (New York: NYU Press, 2012), pp. 159-84.

33. This is more complicated in Augustine. For Augustine, the *saeculum* is primarily a *time:* the "age" between the Fall and the consummation of the kingdom (the eschaton). So technically (and Augustine is not entirely consistent on this point), the *saeculum* is not coincident with creation and temporality as such; it would represent a disfiguration of temporality after the Fall. In short, "the secular" is not equivalent with "this world" if by "this world" we mean *creation.* For instance, one could imagine the work of baking and candlestick making as vocations in a *good* creation — in a prelapsarian world. In that case, such "mundane" work would not be "secular." But if, instead, "this world" refers to the current fallen configuration of creation (*pace* 1 John 2:15-17; 5:19), then the *saeculum* is identical to "this world."

ular" pursuits.[34] Following Taylor, let's call this **secular₁** (*Secular Age,* pp. 1-2).

2. In modernity, particularly in the wake of the Enlightenment, "secular" begins to refer to a nonsectarian, neutral, and *a*religious space or standpoint. The public square is "secular" insofar as it is (allegedly) nonreligious; schools are "secular" when they are no longer "parochial" — hence "public" schools are thought to be "secular" schools. Similarly, in the late twentieth century people will describe themselves as "secular," meaning they have no religious affiliation and hold no "religious" beliefs. We'll refer to this as **secular₂** (pp. 2-3). It is this notion of the secular that is assumed both by the secularization thesis and by normative **secularism**. According to secularization theory, as cultures experience modernization and technological advancement, the (divisive) forces of religious belief and participation wither in the face of modernity's disenchantment of the world. According to secularism, political spaces (and the constitutions that create them) should carve out a realm purified of the contingency, particularity, and irrationality of religious belief and instead be governed by universal, neutral rationality. Secular*ism* is always secularism₂.[35] And secularization theory is usually a confident expectation that societies will be become secular₂ — that is, characterized by decreasing religious belief and participation. People who self-identify as "secular" are usually identifying as areligious.

3. But Taylor helpfully articulates a third sense of the secular (**secular₃**) — and it is this notion that should be heard in his title: *A Secular Age.* A society is secular₃ insofar as religious belief or belief in God is understood to be one option among others, and thus contestable (and con-

---

34. One can thus read the Protestant Reformation as refusing and obliterating the distinction by sacralizing what had been previously construed as merely "secular" (*Secular Age,* pp. 265-66). In short, all is sacred, or at least has the potential of being a sacred vocation if rightly ordered.

35. This is also the secularism that is refused by "postsecular" theorists such as William Connolly in *Why I Am Not a Secularist* (Minneapolis: University of Minnesota Press, 1999).

tested). At issue here is a shift in "the conditions of belief."[36] As Taylor notes, the shift to secularity "in this sense" indicates "a move from a society where belief in God is unchallenged and indeed, unproblematic, to one in which it is understood to be one option among others, and frequently not the easiest to embrace" (p. 3).[37] It is in this sense that we live in a "secular age" even if religious participation might be visible and fervent. And it is in this sense that we could still entertain a certain "secularization$_3$ thesis." But this would be an account, not of how religion will wither in late modern societies, but rather of how and why the plausibility structures of such societies will make religion contestable (and contested).[38] It is the emergence of "the secular" in this sense that makes possible the emergence of an **"exclusive humanism"** — a radically new[39] option in the marketplace of beliefs, a vision

36. Detailing this "shift" is the focus of *Secular Age,* chap. 1.

37. On these criteria, the ancient world into which Christianity emerged — and perhaps *because* Christianity emerged — would have been secular$_3$. So something like modernity may not be a necessary condition for secular$_3$. Granted, the ancient world could not yet have imagined exclusive humanism as a viable option, and that is an important feature of *our* secular age.

38. This seems to be very similar to what Jeffrey Stout — a critic of secular*ism* — describes as the "secularization" of political discourse: "What makes a form of discourse secularized, according to my account, is not the tendency of the people participating in it to relinquish their religious beliefs or to refrain from employing them as reasons. The mark of secularizations, as I use the term, is rather the fact that participants in a given discursive practice are not in a position to take for granted that their interlocutors are making the same religious assumptions they are." Thus participants in such "secularized" discourse "cannot reasonably . . . expect a single theological perspective to be shared by all of their interlocutors." See Stout, *Democracy and Tradition* (Princeton: Princeton University Press, 2004), p. 97. Unfortunately Stout seems to think that those he calls "new traditionalists" (MacIntyre, Hauerwas, and Milbank) "resent" this situation (p. 99), as if they all longed for the reinstitution of Christendom and reversion to the plausibility conditions of the Holy Roman Empire. This is a serious misreading that can't distract us here. But for a relevant discussion, see John Milbank, "A Closer Walk on the Wild Side," in *Varieties of Secularism in a Secular Age,* pp. 54-82.

39. This is not to say that prior ages have been homogenous with respect to belief or religion, only that there was prior contestability between paganism and other axial religions. "Exclusive humanism" could not be thought prior to certain conditions that emerged in modernity. In response to Taylor's critique, Dreyfus and Kelly do not merely try to defend exclusive humanism — they try to return it to a kind of paganism.

of life in which anything beyond the immanent is eclipsed. "For the first time in history a purely self-sufficient humanism came to be a widely available option. I mean by this a humanism accepting no final goals beyond human flourishing, nor any allegiance to anything else beyond this flourishing. Of no previous society was this true" (*Secular Age,* p. 18).

Ours is a secular$_3$ age. While the conditions of secularity — the nonaxiomatic nature of belief in God, the contestability of all ultimate beliefs — are not unrelated to the prescriptive project of secularism$_2$, there is no necessary connection between the two. A secular$_3$ society could undergo religious revival where vast swaths of the populace embrace religious belief. But that could never turn back the clock on secularization$_3$; we would always know we *used* to believe something else, that there are plausible visions of meaning and significance on offer. We would also believe *amidst* the secular$_3$ condition; indeed, conversion is a response to secularity, not an escape from it.

Taylor's driving concern is to help us understand how we got here: What changed? How? What are the effects on belief in a secular age? What are the effects on secularism$_2$ as a cultural project or political ideal? What are the features of the "exclusive humanism" that emerges with the secular$_3$?

> Taylor not only explains *un*belief in a secular age; he also emphasizes that even belief is changed in our secular age. There are still believers who believe the same things as their forebears 1,500 years ago; but *how* we believe has changed. Thus faith communities need to ask: **How does this change in the "conditions" of belief impact the way we proclaim and teach the faith? How does this impact faith formation? How should this change the propagation of the faith for the next generation?**

Taylor's Method: The "Story" of Secularization

Taylor's response to these questions is to tell a story. He is upfront and unapologetic about this. "The narrative is not an optional extra," he insists, which is "why I believe that I have to tell a story here" (p. 29). But why?

He offers at least a couple of reasons. First, he needs to offer a story to counter the "**subtraction stories**" of secularization theory, those tales of enlightenment and progress and maturation that see the emergence of modernity and "the secular" as shucking the detritus of belief and superstition. Once upon a time, as these subtraction stories rehearse it, we believed in sprites and fairies and gods and demons. But as we became rational, and especially as we marshaled naturalist explanations for what we used to attribute to spirits and forces, the world became progressively disenchanted. Religion and belief withered with scientific exorcism of superstition. Natch.[40]

On Taylor's account, the *force* of such subtraction stories is as much in their narrative power as in their ability to account for the "data," so to speak. There is a dramatic tension here, a sense of plot, and a cast of characters with heroes (e.g., Galileo) and villains (e.g., Cardinal Bellarmine). So if you're going to counter subtraction stories, it's not enough to offer rival evidence and data; you need to tell a different *story.* And so Taylor not only "has to tack back and forth between the analytical and the historical" (p. 29), he has to offer the history *as* story, as a counternarrative.

This means that, despite the prosaic verbosity and intellectual detours of the text, one needs to read *A Secular Age* almost like a novel — or at least absorb it *as* a story. Colin Jager rightly appreciates this point as a matter of Taylor's "Romanticism." We need to treat "the book as if it were a literary text — a move itself licensed by the fact that a recognizably modern notion of literariness, as something simultaneously distinct from Christianity and yet remarkably proximate to it, emerges for the first time during the Romantic era."[41] This is because ultimately Taylor wants to try to communicate what it *feels* like to live in a secular age, what it *feels* like to inhabit the cross-pressured space of modernity. Jager thus reformulates Taylor's question in light of this methodology: "What does secularity feel like from the inside?" This changes how we approach the argument: "When Taylor says he has a story to tell, he means that his account must be undergone, not simply paraphrased or glossed."[42]

---

40. This is why he later suggests that this narrative becomes sedimented in the social imaginary of the West, having "sunk to the level of unchallenged common sense" (*Secular Age*, p. 525).

41. Colin Jager, "This Detail, This History: Charles Taylor's Romanticism," in *Varieties of Secularism in a Secular Age,* pp. 166-92, at 168.

42. Jager, "This Detail, This History," p. 173. I will return to Jager's discussion below when we address in what sense *A Secular Age* is an "apologetic."

Second, akin to Alasdair MacIntyre and Christian Smith, Taylor seems to recognize that we are "narrative animals": we define who we are, and what we ought to do, on the basis of what story we see ourselves in. "Our understanding of ourselves and where we stand is partly defined by our sense of having come to where we are, of having overcome a previous condition" (*Secular Age,* p. 28). This is why the historical back story receives such lopsided attention, a fact we'll need to keep in view. While the goal is to understand the present, this requires a long detour through our past. I think this reflects Taylor's Hegelian side — a deep appreciation for the contingencies of history. So we can't tell a neat-and-tidy story of deduction from abstract principles. No, if we're going to make sense of our muddled present, we need to get close to the ground and explore all kinds of contingent twists and turns that are operative in the background of our present. We need to attend to the background of what Jeffrey Stout calls our "dialectical location,"[43] the concrete *particulars* that make us "us," that got us to where we are.[44] This is a bit like realizing that forging a relationship with a significant other requires getting her or his back story; that there is a family history that is embedded in your partner, and understanding the partner requires understanding that story if the relationship is going to move forward.

So the analysis of our secular age begins: "Once upon a time . . ."

43. Stout, *Democracy and Tradition,* p. 79.

44. One can also see this in Taylor's caution about constructing abstract notions of what it means for a society to be "secular." There are no transcendental principles that can be dictated from "above the fray." They need to emerge from the particular vagaries of different social contexts. See Charles Taylor, "Why We Need a Radical Redefinition of Secularism," in *The Power of Religion in the Public Sphere,* ed. Eduardo Mendieta and Jonathan VanAntwerpen (New York: Columbia University Press, 2011), pp. 35-36.

CHAPTER 1

Reforming Belief: The Secular as Modern Accomplishment

More than Subtraction: Obstacles to Unbelief

The "secular" is not just the neutral, rational, areligious world that is left over once we throw off superstition, ritual, and belief in the gods. This is because the secular is not just *un*belief, or lack of specifically religious belief. What characterizes secularity$_3$ — and the secular$_3$ age — is not merely privative. The emergence of the secular is also bound up with the production of a new option — the possibility of exclusive humanism as a viable **social imaginary** — a way of constructing meaning and significance without any reference to the divine or transcendence. So it wasn't enough for us to stop believing in the gods; we also had to be able to *imagine* significance within an immanent frame, to imagine modes of meaning that did not depend on transcendence. This is why "subtraction stories" of the sort offered by secularization theory will always fall short. The secular is not simply a remainder; it is a sum, created by addition, a product of intellectual multiplication.

So, if we're going to answer Taylor's overarching question — How did we get here from there? How did we get from a time (in, say, 1500) in which atheism was virtually unthinkable to a time (in 2000) when theism is almost unbelievable? — we can't simply note when and where various beliefs were knocked off. We also have to consider the change in conditions that made it possible for the West to be able to imagine exclusive humanism as a viable vision of significance.

26

This is where Taylor's story begins. We have to try to imagine the scene: we're in the late medieval world, and atheism is pretty much unthinkable. This certainly doesn't mean everyone believes the same thing. Far from it. In fact, crucial to Taylor's account is the recognition of all kinds of competing visions of Christianity already operative in the West before the Reformation. But still, no one has yet dreamed of Nietzsche or Christopher Hitchens. Why was that? What were those features of the "background" or "imaginary" of medieval society that occluded these imaginative possibilities? If we can identify those features of the medieval social imaginary, we will have located the "obstacles to unbelief" that need to change to make both secularity and exclusive humanism imaginable (*Secular Age*, p. 29). Taylor highlights three features of this medieval imaginary that functioned as obstacles to unbelief (p. 25):

1. The natural world was constituted as a cosmos that functioned semiotically, as a sign that pointed beyond itself, to what was *more* than nature.

2. Society itself was understood as something grounded in a higher reality; earthly kingdoms were grounded in a heavenly kingdom.

3. In sum, people lived in an enchanted world, a world "charged" with presences, that was open and vulnerable, not closed and self-sufficient.

It's not that these features guarantee that all medieval inhabitants "believe in God"; but it does mean that, in a world so constituted, "atheism comes close to being inconceivable" (p. 26) because one can't help but "see" (or "imagine") that world as sort of haunted — suffused with presences that are not "natural." To say this was part of the ancient and medieval imaginary is to say that it's what was taken for granted. So some part of the answer to Taylor's overarching question about how this changed is that "these three features have vanished." Not until these obstacles were removed could something like exclusive humanism emerge.

Our Modern Secular Imaginary: Removing Obstacles to Unbelief

To get at this, we really need to try to *feel* the difference between that age and ours. Because we're not really talking about what people *think;* it's more a matter of the difference between what we take for granted — what we don't give a second thought — and what people of that age took for granted. Because of this, Taylor is at pains to emphasize that he's not merely talking about changes in *ideas* or shifts in theory. "What I am try-ing to describe here," he urges, "is not a theory. Rather my target is our contemporary lived understanding; that is, the way we naïvely take things to be. We might say: the construal we just live in, without ever being aware of it as a construal, or — for most of us — without ever even formulat-ing it" (p. 30). It is at this "level" that the shift has occurred; it is a shift in our naïve understanding, in what we take for granted (pp. 30-31). And this shift to a new "background" is *not* just true for exclusivist humanists; even believers believe in a way that also generally takes for granted this new background. So the shift to a secular age not only makes exclusive humanism a live option for us, it also changes religious communities. We're all secular now.

Taylor lays out five elements of our modern, secular$_3$ social imag-inary, highlighting the contrast with premodern forms of life and the assumptions that attended them. What we'll notice is that each of these elements effectively rejects some aspect of the medieval imaginary we noted above.

Disenchantment and the "Buffered" Modern Self

It is a mainstay of secularization theory that modernity "disenchants" the world — evacuates it of spirits and various ghosts in the machine. Diseases are not demonic, mental illness is no longer possession, the body is no longer ensouled. Generally disenchantment is taken to simply be a matter of naturalization: the magical "spiritual" world is dissolved and we are left with the machinations of matter. But Taylor's account of disenchantment has a different accent, suggesting that this is primarily a shift in the *location* of meaning, moving it from "the world" *into* "the mind."[1] Significance no longer inheres in things; rather, meaning and significance are a property of minds who perceive meaning internally. The external world might be a catalyst for perceiving meaning, but the meanings are generated within the mind — or, in stronger versions (say, Kant), meanings are imposed upon things by minds. Meaning is now located in *agents*. Only once this shift is in place can the proverbial brain-in-a-vat scenario gain any currency; only once meaning is located in minds can we worry that someone or something could completely dupe us about the meaning of the world by manipulating our brains. It is the modern social imaginary that makes it possible for us to imagine *The Matrix*.

To sense the force of this shift, we need to appreciate how this differs from the "enchanted" premodern imaginary where all kinds of nonhuman things *mean* — are loaded and charged with meaning — independent of human perception or attribution. In this premodern, enchanted universe, it was also assumed that *power* resided in things, which is precisely why things like relics or the Host could be invested with spiritual power. As a result, "in the enchanted world, the line between personal agency and impersonal force was not at all clearly drawn" (p. 32). There is a kind of blurring of boundaries so that it is not only personal agents that have causal power (p. 35). Things can do stuff.

At this point Taylor introduces a key concept to describe the premodern self: prior to this disenchantment and the retreat of meaning into an interior "mind," the human agent was seen as porous (p. 35). Just as premodern nature is always already intermixed with its beyond, and just as things are intermixed with mind and meaning, so the premodern self's porosity means the self is essentially *vulnerable* (and hence also "healable"). To be human is to be essentially *open* to an outside (whether benevolent or malevolent), open to blessing or curse, possession or grace. "This sense of vulnerability," Taylor concludes, "is one of the principal features which have gone with disenchantment" (p. 36).

At stake in disenchantment, then, are assumptions not just about meaning but also about minds, about the nature of agents and persons.

---

1. Taylor notes that this is not only about "linguistic meaning" but also about the fuller sense of meaning as in "the meaning of life" (p. 31). This will be related to his later use of the term "fullness," which will be discussed further below.

In the shift to the modern imaginary, minds are "bounded," *inward* spaces. So the modern self, in contrast to this premodern, **porous self**, is a **buffered self**, insulated and isolated in its interiority (p. 37), "giving its own autonomous order to its life" (pp. 38-39).

What does this have to do with our overarching question? Why would this make unbelief so hard in a premodern world? Taylor suggests it yields a "very different existential condition" because in an enchanted, porous world of vulnerable selves, "the prospect of rejecting God does not involve retiring to the safe redoubt of the buffered self, but rather chancing ourselves in the field of forces without him. . . . In general, going against God is not an option in the enchanted world. That is one way the change to the buffered self has impinged" (p. 41). In other words, it wasn't enough to simply divest the world of spirits and demons; it was also necessary that the self be buffered and protected. Not until that positive shift came about did atheism/exclusive humanism become more "thinkable." So this relocation of meaning and its attendant "buffering" of the self removed one of the obstacles to unbelief. Exclusive humanism becomes a little more thinkable.

Living Social

Not only were things invested with significance in the premodern imaginary, but the social bond itself was enchanted, sacred. "Living in the enchanted, porous world of our ancestors was inherently living socially" (p. 42). The good of a common weal is a *collective* good, dependent upon the social rituals of the community. "So we're all in this together." As a result, a premium is placed on *consensus,* and "turning 'heretic' " is "*not* just a personal matter." That is, there is no room for these matters to be ones of "private" preference. "This is something we constantly tend to forget," Taylor notes, "when we look back condescendingly on the intolerance of earlier ages. As long as the common weal is bound up in collectives rites, devotions, allegiances, it couldn't be seen just as an individual's own business that he break ranks, even less that he blaspheme or try to desecrate the rite. There was immense common motivation to bring him back into line" (p. 42). Individual disbelief is not a private option we can grant to heretics to pursue on weekends; to the contrary, disbelief has communal repercussions.

So if there is going to be room to not believe (or believe in exclusive humanism), then this very sociality or communitarianism has to be removed as yet another obstacle. The emergence of the buffered self already lays the groundwork for this since "this understanding lends itself to individuality, even atomism. . . . The buffered self is essentially the self which is aware of the possibility of disengagement" (pp. 41-42). The buffering of the self from alien forces also carves out a space for a nascent privacy, and such privacy provides both protection and permission to disbelieve. Once individuals become the locus of meaning, the social atomism that results means that disbelief no longer has social consequences. "We" are not a seamless cloth, a tight-knit social body; instead, "we" are just a collection of individuals — like individual molecules in a social "gas." This diminishes the ripple effect of individual decisions and beliefs. You're free to be a heretic — which means, eventually, that you're free to be an atheist.

The Carnival Is Over: "Lowering the Bar" for Flourishing

Remember that we are tracking those features of the premodern imaginary that needed to be abolished in order to create room not only for unbelief but also for the positive emergence of exclusive humanism as a live option for organizing both an individual life and whole societies. The buffering of the self protects us from the danger of not believing in the gods; the privatized, individualized self protects us from the social stigma of not being part of the team, so to speak. Taylor identifies a critical third element that we might describe as the mundanization of the *ne plus ultra* — a sort of "lowering of the bar" in how we envision the requirements of a life well lived. Once again, we'll get a feel for this shift if we try to get a sense of how this differs from premodern lived experience.

Especially in Christendom, Taylor recalls, there was a unique tension between "self-transcendence" — a "turning of life towards something *beyond* ordinary human flourishing" — and the this-worldly concerns of human flourishing and creaturely existence. We might redescribe this as a tension between what "eternity" required and what the mundane vagaries of domestic life demanded. It was assumed that human life found its ultimate meaning and telos in a transcendent eternity *and* that the demands of securing such an ultimate life required a certain ascetic relation to the pleasures and demands of mundane, domestic life. The spiritual disciplines of the saint are a lot to ask of the nursemaid or the peasant laborer who is pressed by more immediate concerns. This equates to a tension between "the demands of the total transformation which the faith calls to" and "the requirements of ordinary ongoing human life" (p. 44).[2]

In Christendom this tension is not resolved, but inhabited. First, the social body makes room for a certain division of labor. By making room for entirely "religious" vocations such as monks and nuns, the church creates a sort of vicarious class who ascetically devote themselves to transcendence/eternity *for* the wider social body who have to deal with the nitty-gritty of creaturely life, from kings to peasant mothers (which is why patronage of monasteries and abbeys is an important expression of religious devotion for those otherwise consumed by "worldly" concerns). We miss this if we retroactively impose our "privatized" picture of faith upon abbeys and monasteries and imagine that the monks are devoting themselves to personal pursuits of salvation. The monks pray *for* the world, in the world's stead. So the social body lives this tension between transcendence and the mundane by a kind of division of labor.[3]

Second, the social body in Christendom has a sense of time that allows even those daily engaged in domestic life to nonetheless pursue rhythms and rituals that inhabit this tension between the pressures of now and the hopes of eternity. Rhythms and seasons create opportunities to live the tension (this can be as simple as no meat on Fridays or during Lent). The rituals deal with this tension in order to foster equilibrium. Taylor's most extensive example is Carnival (we get dimmed-down, distorted versions of this in Mardi Gras or Halloween). Carnival

---

2. I do think this is a uniquely "Roman Catholic" framing of the matter and ultimately assumes an implicit understanding of the nature/grace relation. I'm not just saying that the medieval world assumed this Catholic framing, but that *Taylor's* framing it this way also reflects a certain bias in this respect. For example, Protestant heirs of Calvin's vision of "Reform" would see more continuity between the expectations and demands of creational flourishing and eternal flourishing.

3. As we will see momentarily, this vision goes off the rails when those devoted to religious vocations are perceived to be "closer" to the eternal. It is this distortion that generates the project of Reform.

is a sanctioned way to blow off the steam that builds up from the pressure of living under the requirements of eternity. "These were periods in which the ordinary order of things was inverted, or 'the world was turned upside down.' . . . Boys wore the mitre, or fools were made kings for a day; what was ordinarily revered was mocked, people permitted themselves various forms of license, not just sexually but also in close-to-violent acts, and the like" (pp. 45-46). Carnival was a "safety valve": "The weight of virtue and good order was so heavy, and so much steam built up under this suppression of instinct, that there had to be periodic blow-outs if the whole system were not to fly apart" (p. 46). Here again, the equilibrium between mundane demands and eternal requirements is maintained, not by resolving the tension in one direction or another, but by inhabiting the tension. Ideally, the demands and expectations of virtue are not compromised or relaxed or dismissed as untenable — they are just periodically suspended.[4] What society recognized was a need for ritualized "anti-structure" (p. 50).

What changes in modernity is that, instead of inhabiting this tension and trying to maintain an equilibrium between the demands of creaturely life and the expectations for eternal life, the modern age generates different strategies for *resolving* (i.e., eliminating) the tension.[5] There are a couple of options: you can either effectively denounce creaturely domestic life and sort of demand monasticism for all (the so-called puritanical option); or you can drop the expectations of eternity that place the weight of virtue on our domestic lives — that is, you can stop being burdened by what eternity/salvation demands and simply frame ultimate flourishing within *this* world. (Taylor will suggest that modes of Reform that sought to merely clarify the tension and equilibrium actually unleashed the latter option, "resolving" the tension by eliminating it altogether.)

---

4. Taylor notes that this is very different from modern demonstrations and protests. "The festivals were not putting forward an alternative to the established order, in anything like the sense we understand in modern politics, that is, presenting an antithetical order of things which might replace the prevailing dispensation. The mockery was enframed by a [*sic*] understanding that betters, superiors, virtue, ecclesial charisma, etc. ought to rule; the humour was in that sense not ultimately serious" (p. 46).

5. We'll see that the Protestant Reformation, as part of a larger drive for Reform, plays a key role in this shift.

The Fullness of Time

In documenting these shifts from the medieval to the modern imaginary — from enchantment to disenchantment — Taylor also notes a significantly different time-consciousness. In the premodern understanding, because "mundane" or secular$_1$ time is transcended by "higher" time, there is an accounting of time that is not merely linear or chronological. Higher times "introduce 'warps' and seeming inconsistencies in profane time-ordering. Events that were far apart in profane time could nevertheless be closely linked" (p. 55). This is somewhat akin to Kierkegaard's account of "contemporaneity" in *Philosophical Fragments:* "Good Friday 1998 is closer in a way to the original day of the Crucifixion than midsummer's day 1997" (*Secular Age,* p. 55).

Our "encasing" in secular time has changed this, and so we take our experience of time to be "natural" (i.e., *not* a construal): "We have constructed an environment in which we live a uniform, univocal secular time, which we try to measure and control in order to get things done" (p. 59). So nothing "higher" impinges upon our calendars — only the ticktock of *chronos,* and the self-imposed burdens of our "projects."

From Cosmos to Universe

The final aspect of the shift involves our view of the natural world; in the premodern imaginary, we live in a *cosmos,* an ordered whole where the "natural" world hangs within its beyond (p. 60). It's as if the universe has layers, and we are always folded into the middle. If the premodern self is "porous," so too is the premodern cosmos.

In contrast to this, the modern imaginary finds us in a "universe" that has its own kind of order, but it is an immanent order of natural laws rather than any sort of hierarchy of being (p. 60). Taylor significantly expands on this theme later in his argument, and we'll return to it below. At this point, we simply recognize that the shift from cosmos to

Taylor lays out these aspects of the modern social imaginary that are taken for granted and function as the "background" for exclusive humanism. **But in what ways has Christianity also absorbed these shifts? Indeed, are there ways in which Christianity propelled these changes?**

universe — from "creation" to "nature" — makes it possible to now imagine meaning and significance as contained within the universe itself, an autonomous, independent "meaning" that is unhooked from any sort of transcendent dependence.

To set up his story and kick off the narrative, Taylor has tried to enumerate five shifts in the modern imaginary that represent significant changes, not primarily in what we *think* but in what we take for granted — the sort of intuitional background that we assume when we do "think" about things. These are changes in our "imaginary" that most of us would never think about, precisely because they are what we take for granted. Each of these elements targeted, or at least chipped away at, the obstacles to unbelief that made atheism difficult before 1500. However, the removal of obstacles doesn't get us on the move; or, to frame this in terms of subtraction stories: it's not the case that "the secular" is what's left over once you've subtracted these obstacles. So he still hasn't identified any *causal* factors in this story. What we need is a positive account of the engine that drove the positive production of both the secular and exclusive humanism. Taylor locates that engine in "Reform."

Reform: The Fulcrum of Modernity

While there are many "causes" for the shift just documented, Taylor appeals to something like a meta-cause — or perhaps better, an umbrella name for these multiple causes: "**Reform**" (with a capital *R*). This rubric names a range of movements already under way in the late medieval period, and so shouldn't be reduced to the Protestant Reformation. This desire for Reform finds expression in a constellation of movements and developments, including movements internal to Christendom and the Roman Catholic Church, as well as Renaissance humanism.

The Reform movements are generated in the pressure we noted above — that difficult space of unstable equilibrium between the demands of eternal and creaturely life. In particular, Taylor highlights "a profound dissatisfaction with the *hierarchical* equilibrium between lay life and the renunciative vocations" (p. 61, emphasis added). What had been intended as a division of labor between religious and lay vocations had taken on this hierarchical ordering and become a "two-tiered religion" (p. 63), a "multi-speed system" (p. 66) with monks and clergy on a fast track, looking disdainfully at the domestic slowpokes mired in "the things of this world" (even though their labor and profit sustained the monasteries and abbeys). Conversely, because spiritual pressure was sequestered to the religious vocation, the "weight of virtue" was relaxed for the wider populace. Carnival was effectively generalized, and some felt that the laity was being let off the eternal hook.

"Reform" is the overarching moniker Taylor uses to describe an array of movements and initiatives in the late Middle Ages and early modernity — movements that are like the underground river of our secular age. Or perhaps better: these developments in the late Middle Ages unfurled possibilities that wouldn't come to fruition until later in the twentieth century. So Taylor's foray into this foggy past (for most of us) is not an arcane detour; it's the family history we need to make sense of the 1960s — the decade we've never left. As Rusty Reno quipped recently, it's always 1968 somewhere. And Taylor suggests we won't understand 1968 — or 2018 — without some chronological archaeology that takes us back to 1518.

All these Reform movements sought to reform and renew social life to address this "two-tiered" distortion we noted above. While Taylor emphasizes that there were solidly Roman Catholic projects of Reform, one can see why he makes the Protestant Reformation a central, if not pivotal, expression of this (p. 77).[6] At its heart, Reform becomes "a drive to make over the whole society to higher standards" (p. 63) rooted in the conviction that "God is sanctifying us everywhere" (p. 79). Together these

6. At several points Taylor entertains some counterfactual musings, considering whether things could have gone differently with respect to the Reformation. "One can even imagine," for example, "another chain of events, in which at least some important elements of the Reformation didn't have to be driven out of the Catholic Church, and to a denial of the sacraments (which Luther for his part never agreed to) and of the value of tradition (which Luther was not as such against). But it would have required a rather different Rome, less absorbed with its power trip than it has tended to be these last centuries" (p. 75; cp. pp. 76, 78-79). But this would have required both different sensibilities on the part of the Reformers and a different stance on the part of Rome.

commitments begin to propel a kind of perfectionism about society that wouldn't have been imagined earlier. Any gap between the ideal and the real is going to be less and less tolerated, *either* because more is going to be expected of society in terms of general sanctification, *or* because less is going to be expected and self-transcendence will be simply eclipsed. If people aren't meeting the bar, you can either focus on helping people reach higher or you can lower the bar. This is why Reform unleashes both Puritanism *and* the '60s. Insofar as Reform is a reaction to this disequilibrium, it can seek to "solve" the problem in two very different ways — and it will take centuries for this to become clear.

Fundamentally, there is a leveling at work here. Rejecting the "multi-speed" and "two-tiered" models, Reform ratchets up expectation: in Reform movements within Christendom, *everyone* is now expected to live all their lives *coram Deo,* before the face of God. In the language of Saint Paul, they are expected to do *all* for the glory of God (Col. 3:17). This is actually the flip side of a new sanctification of "ordinary life" — a refusal of sacred/profane distinctions and the beginning of the erosion of the sacred/secular distinction. Domestic life is affirmed as a sphere of grace. It's not just priests and nuns who are "religious"; the butcher, the baker, and the candlestick maker can also undertake their mundane, "this-worldly" tasks with a sense of devotion and worship.

The result is that "for the ordinary householder" this will "require something paradoxical: living in all the practices and institutions of ['this-worldly'] flourishing, but at the same time not fully in them. Being in them but not of them; being in them, but yet at a distance, ready to lose them. Augustine put it: use the things of this world, but don't enjoy them; uti, not frui. Or do it all for the glory of God, in the Loyola-Calvin formulation" (p. 81). Religious devotion — and hence expectations of holiness and virtue — is not sequestered to the monastery or the convent; rather, the high expectations of sanctification now spill beyond the walls of the monastery.[7]

This is expressed in a couple of ways: on the one hand, ordinary, do-

---

7. Matthew Myer Boulton outlines John Calvin's vision for all of Geneva as a *magna monasterium* in *Life in God: John Calvin, Practical Formation, and the Future of Protestant Theology* (Grand Rapids: Eerdmans, 2011).

mestic life is taken up and sanctified; on the other hand, renunciation is built into ordinary life (p. 81). So the butcher, the baker, and the candlestick maker are affirmed in their "worldly" stations as also called to serve God, just like the priest; on the other hand, the domestic laborer does this with something of a mendicant asceticism.[8] In this sense, "Protestantism is in the line of continuity with mediaeval reform, attempting to raise general standards, not satisfied with a world in which only a few integrally fulfill the gospel, but trying to make certain pious practices absolutely general" (p. 82).

This version of Reform "levels" two-tiered religion by actually expecting everyone to live up to the high expectations of disciplined, monastic life. But Taylor hints that another sort of leveling is possible: you could also solve the two-tiered problem by lifting the weight of virtue, disburdening a society of the expectations of transcendence, and thus lop off the upper tier or the eternal horizon. In fact, he seems to suggest that it was the first strategy of higher expectations that might have driven some to the latter strategy of lowered expectations. By railing against vice and "crank[ing] up the terrifying visions of damnation," Protestant preachers effectively prepared "the desertion of a goodly part of their flock to humanism" (p. 75).[9] One strategy of leveling the two-tier problem might occasion a very different strategy that would ultimately become exclusive humanism.

Disenchantment Redux

Coupled with this leveling was the Reformation's "radical simplification," as Taylor describes it (p. 77). The Reformers "all see the reigning equilibrium as a bad compromise" — a Pelagian assumption of human powers and thus an inadequate appreciation for the radical grace of God and for God's action in salvation. If anything of salvation is under our control, then God's sovereignty and grace are compromised. This leads Reformers like Calvin to reject the "localization" of grace in things and

8. This, of course, is the "innerworldly ascetism" that Max Weber said characterized the "Protestant ethic." Taylor discusses this in much more detail in *Sources of the Self* (Cambridge: Harvard University Press, 1989), pp. 211-33.

9. This is not an uncontroversial hypothesis.

rituals, changing the "centre of gravity of the religious life" (p. 79). Taylor considers John Calvin as a case study: in emphasizing the priority of God's action and grace, Taylor notes, "what he can't admit is that God could have released something of his saving efficacy out there into the world, at the mercy of human action, because that is the cost of really sanctifying creatures like us which are bodily, social, historical" (p. 79). It is the (relatively immaterial) spoken Word of God and not magical things like the Host that is the means of grace.[10]

One can see how this entails a kind of *dis*enchantment: "we reject the sacramentals; all the elements of 'magic' in the old religion" (p. 79). If the church no longer has "good" magic, "then all magic must be black" (p. 80); all enchantment must be blasphemous, idolatrous, even demonic (Salem is yet to come). And once the world is disenchanted and de-charged of transcendence, we are then free to reorder it as seems best (p. 80). In other words, the Reformers' rejection of sacramentalism is the beginning of naturalism, or it at least opens the door to its possibility. It is also the beginning of a certain evacuation of the sacred as a *presence* in the world. And that leads to a completely new understanding of social and cultural life as well. Social and political arrangements are no longer enchanted givens; the king or monarch can't be any sort of "sacramental" reality. There is no enchanted social order. If the world is going to be ordered, *we* need to do it.[11] "We feel a new free-

Taylor's account celebrates the Reformation's "sanctification of ordinary life" while also suggesting that this was the camel's nose in the tent of enchantment — that somehow the Protestant Reformation opened the door to what would become, by a winding, contingent path, exclusive humanism. **Are there ways that Protestants can recognize this mixed legacy of the Reformation and yet also affirm it as a renewal movement within the church catholic? If the Protestant Reformation opened a door to exclusive humanism, did it not also open the door that led to Vatican II?**

---

10. Whether this is a fair reading of Calvin's sacramental theology is debatable. See Laura Smit, " 'The Depth behind Things': Toward a Calvinist Sacramental Theology," in *Radical Orthodoxy and the Reformed Tradition*, ed. James K. A. Smith and James H. Olthuis (Grand Rapids: Baker Academic, 2005), pp. 205-27. However, this is certainly true of the de-sacramentalized heirs of Calvin following Zwingli, etc.

11. See Michael Walzer, *Revolution of the Saints: A Study in the Origins of Radical Politics*

dom in a world shorn of the sacred, and the limits it set for us, to re-order things as seems best. We take the crucial stance, for faith and glory of God. Acting out of this, we order things for the best. . . . A great energy is released to re-order affairs in secular time" (p. 80).

It was this "rage for order," Taylor suggests, that unwittingly contributed to the disenchantment of the world: "This, plus the inherent drive of the religious reformations, made them work towards the disenchantment of the world, and the abolition of society based on hierarchical equilibrium, whether that of élite and mass, or that we find reflected in the Carnival, and the 'world turned upside down' " (p. 87). It is religious Reform that calls for secular reform, which in turn makes possible exclusively humanist reform. The Reformation has some explaining to do.[12]

Creation, Nature, and Incarnation:
A Zigzag Path to Exclusive Humanism

Taylor reemphasizes an important point: the path from 1500 to 2000 is not a straight shot. As he's said before, this is not just a "subtraction" story, a linear narrative of inevitable "progress." Subtraction stories are straight-shot accounts that assume the truth and goodness of the terminus, and thus simply read developments as steps on the way to that end (p. 90). In contrast, highlighting the complexity of causes and the contingency of different developments, Taylor offers a "zigzag account" that recognizes a contingent sort of pinball effect. The point is that developments that, *from our (modern, secularist) perspective,* might seem to be "advances" toward our secular accomplishment, "in other circumstances might never have come to have the meaning that [they bear] for unbelievers today" (p. 95). Our anachronistic hindsight tends to impose a secularist trajectory on earlier shifts whereas, in fact, they might have been "pointed" in a very different direction.

(Cambridge: Harvard University Press, 1965). For relevant discussion, see Nicholas Wolterstorff, *Until Justice and Peace Embrace* (Grand Rapids: Eerdmans, 1983), chap. 1.

12. For a significant expansion on this theme, see Brad S. Gregory, *The Unintended Reformation: How a Religious Revolution Secularized Society* (Cambridge: Harvard University Press, Belknap Press, 2012).

Taylor's case in point here is a shift to a new interest in "nature," or more specifically, nature "for its own sake" (p. 90). Now, from the vantage point of secular humanism, this new interest in nature can look like the next logical step on the way to pure immanence: first distinguish God/ nature, then disenchant, then be happy and content with just nature and hence affirm the autonomy and sufficiency of nature. Such a story about the "autonomization" of nature posits a contrast or dichotomy between belief in God and interest in "nature-for-itself" (p. 91).

The only problem with such a story is that it fails to account for two important historical realities: (1) it was precisely *Christians* who were exhibiting a new interest in creation/nature *for theological reasons;* and (2) this interest was clearly not mutually exclusive with belief in God and an affirmation of transcendence. In particular, the late medieval and Renaissance investment in nature, embodiment, and particularity is rooted in a new incarnational spirituality (pp. 93ff.). This was very much an "evangelical" development, concerned with bringing Christ to the world, and thus recognizing God's own "incarnational" move in that re- gard — meeting humanity where it is, in bodies, history, etc. — so clearly evident in art from this period. "So it is not altogether surprising that this attempt to bring Christ to the world, the lay world, the previously unhal- lowed world, should inspire a new focus on this world" (p. 94). This was primarily a revolution in devotion, not metaphysics. Thus "the new inter- est in nature was not a step outside of a religious outlook, even partially; it was a mutation within this outlook" (p. 95). While this shift might, from a later vantage point, *look* like the first step toward exclusive humanism and pure immanence, it was not at the beginning — and *could* have gone otherwise.[13] "That the autonomy of nature eventually . . . came to serve as grist to the mill of exclusive humanism is clearly true," Taylor concludes. "That establishing it was already a step in that direction is profoundly false" (p. 95).

True to his zigzag account of causal complexity, Taylor notes another development, roughly parallel to the incarnational emphasis: the rise of

13. Though we should also recognize that "the Renaissance" is not a homogenous move- ment either. Even Ruskin, in *Stones of Venice,* recognized two renaissances — the sort that Ruskin and Taylor celebrate, but also the renaissance of Walter Pater and Oscar Wilde.

nominalism, which *is* a metaphysical thesis. Taylor notes that nominalism was not a proto-secularism precisely because the motives behind nominalism were fundamentally theological. In particular, nominalism arose as a way of metaphysically honoring a radical sense of God's sovereignty and power. At issue for nominalists like Scotus was something like this: the Aristotelian notion of a human "nature" saw the good of the human being determined by the *nature* or *telos* of the human being; so there was a defined way to be good. Now while God the Creator might have created this telos or nature, once created it would seem to actually put a constraint on God, since enabling humans to achieve their (good) end would require that God sort of "conform" to this good/telos. "But this seemed to some thinkers an unacceptable attempt to limit God's sovereignty. God must always remain free to determine what is good." So if one were going to preserve God's absolute sovereignty, one would have to do away with "essences," with independent "natures." And the result is a metaphysical picture called "nominalism" where things are only what they are *named* (*nom*-ed) (p. 97).

"But if this is right," Taylor comments, "then we, the dependent, created agents, have also to relate to these things not in terms of the normative patterns they reveal, but in terms of the autonomous super-purposes of our creator [which can't be known a priori]. The purposes things serve are extrinsic to them. The stance is fundamentally one of instrumental reason" (p. 97). Part of the fallout of such a metaphysical shift is the loss of final causality (a cause that attracts or "pulls"), eclipsing any teleology for things/nature. Understanding something is no longer a matter of understanding its "essence" and hence its telos (end). Instead we get the "mechanistic" universe that we still inhabit today, in which *efficient* causality (a cause that "pushes") is the only causality and can only be discerned by empirical observation. This, of course, is precisely the assumption behind the scientific method as a way of divining the efficient causes of things, not by discerning "essence" but by empirical observation of patterns, etc. The result is nothing short of "a new understanding of being, according to which, all intrinsic purposes having been expelled, final causation drops out, and efficient causation alone remains" (p. 98).

But keep in mind Taylor's zigzag point: the incarnational interest in nature is not necessarily a step on the way to the autonomization of nature; rather, only when it is "mixed" with another development, nominalism, does it seem to head in that direction. There is a sort of intellectual chemical reaction between the two that generates a by-product that neither on its own would have generated — or would have wanted. Taylor is emphasizing the contingency of these developments: *it could have been otherwise,* and without the triumph of nominalism we might have had a very different concern with nature for its own sake.

Taylor sees a kind of parallel "autonomization" of nature in the realm of ethics and politics, expressed in the goal of "civility" (p. 99), which is a concern to *manage* our passions and social life. Civility becomes a sort of naturalized, secularized sanctification. "Civility was not something you attained at a certain stage in history, and then relaxed into"; rather, "civility requires working on yourself, not just leaving things as they are, but making them over. It involves a struggle to reshape ourselves" (pp. 100, 101). This required *disciplines,* and such disciplined citizens would also be contributors to the common good (especially in terms of productivity). This really translated into a program of *self*-discipline (p. 111), an internalization of discipline, while also contributing to the development of the "police state" — statecraft *as* discipline (pp. 110-11). Again Taylor notes a link between metaphysics and politics, ontology and statecraft: if nominalism is true, "not only must we alter our model of science — no longer the search for Aristotelian or Platonic form, it must search for relations of efficient causality; but the manipulable universe invites us to develop a Leistungswissen, or a science of control" (p. 113). The result is a monster: a Christianized neo-Stoicism that appends a deity to Stoic emphases on action and control. "Neo-Stoicism is the zig to which Deism will be the zag" (p. 117).

So religious expectations of sanctification are increasingly generalized, yielding a new vision of how society can and should be ordered. But there is a corresponding shift in religious practice that must also be noted. These developments — de-sacramentalization and the generalization of "discipline" — come with the "eclipse" of other key features of premodern Christian religion. In particular, Taylor highlights the loss of any coherent place for *worship:* "the eclipse of certain crucial Christian elements, those of grace and of agape, already changed quite decisively the centre of gravity of this outlook. Moreover, there didn't seem to be an essential place for the worship of God, other than through the cultivation of reason and constancy" (p. 117). It is in this context that the apologetic and polemic edge of Taylor's argument can be felt. Indeed, one might get a sense that he's taking sides in an intramural debate within Christianity when he acerbically notes that "this silence could be seen as an invitation to belong to 'the church of your choice' " — a quintessentially Protestant notion of the church as a voluntary association. Perhaps it's no accident that it is Taylor the Roman Catholic who sees in these developments "a relegation of worship as ultimately unnecessary and irrelevant" (p. 117). We will encounter these themes again when he introduces the notion of **"excarnation"** as an effect of Reform.

Again, there are no straight shots here, no simply straightforward paths of inevitable "progress" from magic to modernity, from disruptive transcendence to ordered immanence. Instead there are multiple shifts and turns, zigs and zags, which could have gone otherwise but — given certain historical contingencies — generated the possibility of exclusive humanism and secularity as we know it. To appreciate how *un*-inevitable this was, we need to try to imagine the messiness of these tensions and conflicts in an age of upheaval. So Taylor summarizes the point: "A way of putting our present condition [our 'secular age'] is to say that many people are happy living for goals which are purely immanent; they live in a way that takes no account of the transcendent" (p. 143). So what made that possible? How did we get here? Well, it turns out that this was made possible by *theological* shifts associated with movements of Reform. Once we learned to *distinguish* transcendent from immanent, "it eventually became possible to see the immediate surroundings of our lives as existing on this 'natural' plane, however much we might believe that they indicated something beyond" (p. 143). Even Christians, we might say, became functionally disenchanted.

But we cannot anachronistically impose the accomplishment of secular humanism as the necessary end of such a shift. Indeed, Taylor sees such overconfidence as failing to note an irony: the "naturalization" that is essential to exclusive humanism was first motivated by Christian devotion.[14] "The irony is that just this, so much the fruit of devotion and faith,

---

14. Taylor considers the emergence of "realism" in Renaissance Italian and later Nether-

prepares the ground for an escape from faith, into a purely immanent world" (p. 145).

On Taylor's account, these aren't just idle metaphysical speculations; these shifts in the social imaginary of the West make an impact on how we imagine ourselves — how we imagine "we." The "buffered" individual becomes sedimented in a social imaginary, not just part of some social "theory." What emerges, then, is "a new self-understanding of our social existence, one which gave an unprecedented primacy to the individual" (p. 146). It's how we functionally imagine ourselves — it's the picture of our place in the world that we assume without asking. It's exactly the picture we take for granted.

Taylor describes this shift — in which society will come to be seen as a collection of individuals (p. 146) — as "the great disembedding." But we can only make sense of this claim about *dis*embedding if we appreciate the *em*bedding that it's dissing, so to speak. Most germane to understanding the point of this chapter is appreciating what Taylor calls the "triple embedding" of premodern societies, a configuration of society that goes along with what he's been calling enchantment: "Human agents are embedded in society, society in the cosmos, and the cosmos incorporates the divine" (p. 152).[15] The *dis*embedding, then, happens gradually by targeting different facets of this triple embedding (e.g., disenchantment targets the third aspect; social contract theory targets the second aspect; etc.).

This disembedded, buffered, individualist view of the self seeps into our social imaginary — into the very way that we imagine the world, well before we ever *think* reflectively about it. We absorb it with our mother's milk, so to speak, to the extent that it's very difficult for us to imagine the

---

lands painting as a case in point: "the realism, tenderness, physicality, particularity of much of this painting . . . instead of being read as a turning away from transcendence, should be grasped in a devotional context, as a powerful affirmation of the Incarnation" (p. 144). And yet by so investing the material world with significance, these movements also gave immanence a robustness and valorization that no longer seemed to need the transcendent to "suspend" it. In other words, the work of art that could be "iconic" — a window to the transcendent — becomes so fixating in its naturalistic realism that it absorbs our entire gaze and interest and ends up functioning as an idol. For an example of such a reading of Renaissance art, see Jean-Luc Marion, *The Crossing of the Visible,* trans. James K. A. Smith (Stanford: Stanford University Press, 2004), especially his discussion of Caravaggio.

15. Note how he suggests that creation *ex nihilo* already breaks this chain (p. 152).

world otherwise: "once we are well installed in the modern social imaginary, it seems the only possible one" (p. 168). And yet, Taylor's point is that this is an *imaginary* — not that this is all just a fiction, but rather that this is a "**take**" on the world. While we have come to assume that this is just "the way things are," in fact what we take for granted is contingent and contestable. But before we can contest it, we need to further understand it.

CHAPTER 2

The Religious Path to Exclusive Humanism: From Deism to Atheism

How, in a relatively short period of time, did we go from a world where belief in God was the default assumption to our secular age in which belief in God seems, to many, unbelievable? This brave new world is not just the old world with the God-supplement lopped off; it's not just the world that is left when we subtract the supernatural. A secular world where we have permission, even encouragement, to *not* believe in God is an accomplishment, not merely a remainder. Our secular age is the product of creative new options, an entire reconfiguration of meaning.

So it's not enough to ask how we got permission to stop believing in God; we need to also inquire about what emerged to replace such belief. Because it's not that our secular age is an age of *dis*belief; it's an age of believing otherwise. We can't tolerate living in a world without meaning. So if the transcendence that previously gave significance to the world is lost, we need a new account of meaning — a new "imaginary" that enables us to imagine a meaningful life within this now self-sufficient universe of gas and fire. That "replacement" imaginary is what Taylor calls "exclusive humanism," and his quarry is still to discern just how exclusive humanism became a "live option" in modernity (p. 222), resisting typical subtraction stories that posit that "once religious and metaphysical beliefs fall away, we are left with ordinary human desires, and these are the basis of our modern humanism" (p. 253). This is an important point, and we won't understand Taylor's critique of subtraction stories without appreciating it: on the subtraction-story account, modern exclusive humanism is just the natural telos of human life. We are released to be the exclusive humanists we were meant to be when we escape the traps of superstition and the yoke of transcendence. On such tellings of the story, exclusive humanism is "natural." But Taylor's point in part 2 of *A Secular Age* is to show that we had to *learn* how to be exclusively humanist; it is a second nature, not a first.

So what made that possible?

Enclosure and Immanentization: Relocating Significance

As we've already seen, often the features of our secular age were generated from religious and theological moves. Taylor sees a *theological* shift in the understanding of Providence in early modernity that, in turn, leads to an *anthropological* (or even anthropocentric) shift in four movements. Anticipating how Taylor will describe this later, we might see this as a fourfold process of **"immanentization"** — a subtle process by which our world, and hence the realm of significance, is enclosed within the material universe and the natural world. Divested of the transcendent, *this* world is invested with ultimacy and meaning in ways that couldn't have been imagined before. Taylor sees this reflected in four "eclipses" that are domino effects of this process.

The first, and most significant, is an eclipse of what he calls a "further purpose" or a good that "transcends human flourishing."[1] In the premodern, enchanted social imaginary, there was an end for humans that transcended "mundane" flourishing "in this world," so to speak. As he puts

---

1. Though I think Taylor formulates this infelicitously. Because he seems to limit "human flourishing" to "this-worldly" or "mundane" flourishing, he ends up positing a tension between *creaturely* goods and *eternal* goods; that is, he ends up creating a tension between the order of creation and the order of redemption — between nature and grace. I think this is a hangover of a certain type of scholastic Thomism. In the Protestant and Reformed tradition, we would emphasize a fundamental continuity between nature and grace, creation and redemption, even if redemption is also always "more" than creation. So whatever "ascetic" disciplines are required of us "in this life" are not repressions of flourishing but rather constraints *for* our flourishing.

it elsewhere, "For Christians, God wills human flourishing, but 'thy will be done' doesn't reduce to 'let human beings flourish.' "[2] In short, both agents and social institutions lived with a sense of a telos that was eternal — a final judgment, the beatific vision, etc. And on Taylor's accounting, this "higher good" was in some tension with mundane concerns about flourishing (recall his earlier point concerning equilibrium). This entailed a sense of obligation "beyond" human flourishing. In other words, this life is *not* "all there is" — and recognizing that means one lives this life differently. It will engender certain ascetic constraints, for example: we can't just eat, drink, and be merry because, while tomorrow we may die, that's not the end. After that comes the judgment. And so our merriment might be curtailed by this "further purpose," as Taylor describes it.

But Taylor sees an important shift in this respect, particularly in the work of Adam Smith and John Locke, among others. Whereas historically the doctrine of providence assured a benign *ultimate* plan for the cosmos, with Locke and Smith we see a new emphasis: providence is primarily about ordering *this* world for mutual benefit, particularly *economic* benefit. Humans are seen as fundamentally engaged in an "exchange of services," so the entire cosmos is seen anthropocentrically as the arena for this economy (*Secular Age*, p. 177). What happens in the "new Providence," then, is a "shrinking" of God's purposes, an "economizing" of God's own interests: "God's goals for us shrink to the single end of our encompassing this order of mutual benefit he has designed for us" (p. 221). So even our theism becomes humanized, immanentized, and the telos of God's providential concern is circumscribed within immanence. And this becomes true even of "orthodox" folk: "even

Many evangelicals are reacting to the "dualism" of their fundamentalist heritage that seemed to *only* value "heaven" and offered no functional affirmation of the importance of "this life." Their rejection of this finds expression in a new emphasis on "the goodness of creation" and the importance of social justice. **Are there ways that such developments are a delayed replay of the "eclipse of heaven"? Might Taylor's account be a cautionary tale?**

2. Charles Taylor, "A Catholic Modernity?" in *Believing Scholars: Ten Catholic Intellectuals*, ed. James L. Heft, S.M. (New York: Fordham University Press, 2005), p. 17. But as I noted above, I think Taylor is positing something of a false dichotomy here.

people who held to orthodox beliefs were influenced by this humanizing trend; frequently the transcendent dimension of their faith became less central" (p. 222).[3] Because eternity is eclipsed, the this-worldly is amplified and threatens to swallow all.

Taylor describes the second aspect of this anthropocentric shift as the "eclipse of grace." Since God's providential concern for order is reduced to an "economic" ordering of creation to our mutual benefit, and since that order and design is discernible by reason, then "by reason and discipline, humans could rise to the challenge and realize it." The result is a kind of intellectual Pelagianism: we can figure this out without assistance. Oh, God still plays a role — as either the watchmaker who got the ball rolling, or the judge who will evaluate how well we did — but in the long middle God plays no discernible role or function, and is uninvolved (pp. 222-23). This is why Taylor describes all these as features of a "providential *deism*" — a deism that opened the door for exclusive humanism.

Since what matters is immanent, and since we can figure it out, it's not surprising that, third, "the sense of mystery fades." God's providence is no longer inscrutable; it's an open book, "perspicuous." "His providence consists simply in his plan for us, which we understand" (p. 223). Mystery can no longer be tolerated.

Finally, and as an outcome, we lose any "idea that God was planning a transformation of human beings which would take them beyond the limitations which inhere in their present condition" (p. 224). We lose a sense that humanity's end transcends its current configurations — and thus lose a sense of "participation" in God's nature (or "deification") as the telos for humanity.

But what underlay these shifts? Again, Taylor emphasizes economic-centric *harmony* as the new focus and ideal: "The spreading doctrines of the harmony of interests reflect the shift in the idea of natural order . . . ,

---

3. This point seems germane to contemporary evangelicalism, which is increasingly casting off its "otherworldly" piety and becoming newly invested in the flourishing of this world. (For a winsome encapsulation of this, see N. T. Wright, *Surprised by Hope: Rethinking Heaven, the Resurrection, and the Mission of the Church* [San Francisco: HarperOne, 2008].) Taylor's point is that even orthodox Christians unwittingly absorbed this immanentizing, anthropocentric shift. For articulation of this concern, see Hans Boersma, *Heavenly Participation: The Weaving of a Sacramental Tapestry* (Grand Rapids: Eerdmans, 2010).

in which the economic dimension takes on greater and greater importance, and 'economic' (that is, ordered, peaceful, productive) activity is more and more the model for human behaviour" (p. 229). Like the roof on Toronto's SkyDome, the heavens are beginning to close. But we barely notice, because our new focus on this plane had already moved the transcendent to our peripheral vision at best. We're so taken with the play on this field, we don't lament the loss of the stars overhead.

How Apologetics Diminishes Christianity

In this context Taylor offers an analysis of the apologetic strategy that emerges in the midst of these shifts — not only as a response to them, but already as a reflection *of* them. In trying to assess just how the modern social imaginary came to permeate a wider culture, Taylor focuses on Christian responses *to* this emerging humanism and the "eclipses" we've just noted. What he finds is that the responses themselves have already conceded the game; that is, the responses to this diminishment of transcendence already accede to it in important ways (Taylor will later call this "pre-shrunk religion" [p. 226]). As he notes, "the great apologetic effort called forth by this disaffection itself narrowed its focus so drastically. It barely invoked the saving action of Christ, nor did it dwell on the life of devotion and prayer, although the seventeenth century was rich in this. The arguments turned exclusively on demonstrating God as Creator, and showing his Providence" (p. 225). What we get in the name of "Christian" defenses of transcendence, then, is "a less theologically elaborate faith" that, ironically, paves the way for exclusive humanism. God is reduced to a Creator and religion is reduced to morality (p. 225). The "deism" of providential deism bears many marks of the "theism" that is often defended in contemporary apologetics. The particularities of specifically *Christian* belief are diminished to try to secure a more generic deity — as if saving *some* sort of transcendence will suffice.[4]

When Taylor broached this theme earlier, he specifically noted that

4. Taylor notes that specifics of Christology also recede in importance in light of this: "insofar as the figure of Christ, as divine, stands behind claims to sacral authority, while the issue of whether Jesus was God or simply a great prophet or teacher is not relevant to the question whether God is the Designer of the order of mutual benefit, there is a temp-

the "religion" that is defended by such apologetic strategies has little to do with religion in terms of *worship:* "the eclipse of certain crucial Christian elements, those of grace and agape, already changed quite decisively the centre of gravity of this outlook. Moreover, there didn't seem to be any essential place for the worship of God, other than through the cultivation of reason and constancy." What we see, then, is the "relegation of worship as ultimately unnecessary and irrelevant" (p. 117). This is the scaled-down religion that will be rejected "by Wesley from one direction, and later secular humanists from the other" (p. 226).

There is also an important epistemological concession already at work in apologetic responses to immanentization. This mode of "Christian" apologetics bought into the spectatorish "world picture" of the new modern order. Rather than seeing ourselves positioned within a hierarchy of forms (in which case we wouldn't be surprised if "higher levels" are mysterious and inscrutable), we now adopt a God-like, dispassionate "gaze" that deigns to survey the whole. In this mode, the universe appears "as a system before our gaze, whereby we can grasp the whole in a kind of tableau" (p. 232). And it is precisely in this context, when we adopt a "disengaged stance," that the project of *theodicy* ramps up; thinking we're positioned to see everything, we now expect an answer to whatever puzzles us, including the problem of evil. Nothing should be inscrutable.

But this apologetic project — particularly with respect to the "problem" of evil — is taken up in a way that is completely consistent with the "buffered self" (p. 228); while earlier the terrors and burdens of evil and disaster would have cast us upon the help of a Savior, "now that we think we see how it all works, the argument gets displaced. People in coffeehouses and salons [and philosophy classes?] begin to express their disaffection in reflections on divine justice, and the theologians begin to feel that this is the challenge they must meet to fight back the coming wave of unbelief. The burning concern with theodicy is enframed by the new imagined epistemic predicament" (p. 233).[5]

---

tation to abandon either the question or the doctrine of Christ's divinity, to slide towards Socinism, or Deism; or else to adopt a skeptical stance towards such questions" (p. 238).

5. It's very difficult for me to resist recognizing how much of the "industry" of Christian philosophy and apologetics today remains the outcome of these shifts. Just compare Christian responses to the "new atheists" that, in a similar way, have already conceded the

Here's where Taylor's "irony" comes into play: What's left of/for God after this deistic shift? Well, "God remains the Creator, and hence our benefactor ... but this Providence remains exclusively general: particular providences, and miracles, are out" (p. 233). In other words, God plays a function within a system that generally runs without him. "But having got this far," Taylor concludes, "it is not clear why something of the same inspiring power cannot come from the contemplation of the order of nature itself, without reference to a Creator" (p. 234). The scaled-down God and preshrunk religion defended by the apologists turned out to be insignificant enough to reject without consequence. In other words, once God's role is diminished to that of a deistic agent (*by his defenders,* we should add), the gig is pretty much up: "And so exclusive humanism could take hold, as more than a theory held by a tiny minority, but as a more and more viable spiritual outlook. ... The points at which God had seemed an indispensable source for this ordering power were the ones which began to fade and become invisible. The hitherto unthought became thinkable" (p. 234).[6]

The Next Step: The Politics of "Polite" Society

"But not yet thought," Taylor concedes (p. 234). Think*able.* For exclusive humanism to become a "live option," there also had to be a *political* shift, one that mirrors or parallels the theological shift. Just as we noted the move to a "less theologically elaborate" (i.e., less determinate, specified, embodied, *practiced*) religion, so also the political order will be liberated from any particular magisterium. The **"modern moral order,"** as

---

game to exclusive humanism by playing on their turf. Or consider how much "Christian" philosophy is content to be "theistic" philosophy. That said, in a way, my colleague Stephen Wykstra's work on skeptical arguments from evil has pushed back against just this epistemic expectation of being able to "see" everything. See, for example, Stephen J. Wykstra, "The Humean Obstacle to Evidential Arguments from Suffering: On Avoiding the Evils of 'Appearance,'" *International Journal for Philosophy of Religion* 16 (1984): 73-93; Wykstra, "Rowe's Noseeum Arguments from Evil," in *The Evidential Argument from Evil,* ed. Daniel Howard-Snyder (Bloomington: Indiana University Press, 1996), pp. 126-50.

6. In this context, Taylor cites Michael Buckley's classic study, *At the Origins of Modern Atheism* (New Haven: Yale University Press, 1990).

Taylor often calls it, which amounts to an ordering of society for mutual benefit ("economy"), will come to reflect the generic nature of this religion. Unhooked from the specifics of Christian doctrines and tethered to a more generic deistic god, the modern moral order is independent of any specific — and hence contestable — claims about this god. If the generic religion of the apologists is "independent from ecclesiastical or particular-doctrinal authority," then the state and political life can be similarly liberated. "This didn't have to mean, of course, independence from religion; because one could easily conceive of the modern moral order in a providentialist framework, as God's design for humans, as I have described it above. But this just strengthens the point: to see the order as God's design gives it an authority which cannot be overturned by the deliverances of any magisterium, nor set aside in the name of any doctrine particular to one or other denomination" (p. 237).[7] What we have, in other words, is the making of a "civil religion," rooted in a "natural" religion, which can allegedly transcend denominational strife. (Welcome to America!) The ultimate and transcendent are retained but marginalized and made increasingly irrelevant. Our differences about the ultimate fade in comparison to the common project of pursuing the "order of mutual benefit."[8]

What emerges from this is what Taylor describes as "polite society," a new mode of self-sufficient sociality that becomes an end in itself.

> Polite civilization, and the moral order it entrenches, can easily become lived as a self-sufficient framework within which to find the standards of our social, moral and political life; the only transcendent references

---

7. Those forms of religion that refuse to play by these rules will be those that continue to hold an "ideal of sociality" and "sacral authority" identified with the Catholic Church or "high" interpretations of authority in the Church of England. (Which would also anticipate how uneasily some forms of Islam would sit within this imaginary.) "The actual coming-to-be of a range of non-Christian and anti-Christian positions, ranging from various forms of Deism and Unitarianism to exclusive humanism, can best be understood within this field of potential and frequently actualized conflict" (p. 238).

8. An honest assessment of this would have to reckon with the fact that this Hobbesian and Lockean strategy did seem to alleviate the "wars of religion" that beset early modern Europe. For an argument of this point, see Ephraim Radner, *A Brutal Unity: The Spiritual Politics of the Christian Church* (Waco, Tex.: Baylor University Press, 2012).

admitted being those which underpin the order and do not justify in-
fringing it. On the social and civilizational level, it fits perfectly with,
indeed expresses, what I called above the "buffered identity," the self-
understanding which arises out of disenchantment. Otherwise put, it is
a social and civilizational framework which inhibits or blocks out certain
of the ways in which transcendence has historically impinged on humans,
and been present in their lives. It tends to complete and entrench on a
civilizational level the anthropocentric shift I described in the previous
section. It builds for the buffered identity a buffered world. (pp. 238-39)

On the one hand, Taylor regularly describes these moves as reductive:
shrinking, scaling down, lowering the bar, etc. On the other hand, such
"shrinking" is not experienced as a subtraction, as if we are left with less.
To the contrary, the scaling down to immanence actually amplifies its
importance. The immanent sphere — the this-worldly plane — swells in
importance just to the extent that the eternal and the transcendent are
eclipsed. So there's no lament here; if anything, there is new confidence,
excitement, and celebration. Look what *we* can do!

The epistemic Pelagianism we noted above (the confidence that *we*
can figure everything out) is now complemented by a civilizational or cultural Pelagianism: the confidence that *we* make *this* world meaningful.
"Once the goal is shrunk," Taylor observes, "it can begin to seem that we
can encompass it with our unaided forces. Grace seems less essential"
(p. 244). And now we can begin to see how exclusive humanism might
arise: "The stage is set, as it were, for its entrance." But the negative permission (we don't seem to need grace anymore) does not seem a sufficient
condition for its emergence. There also needs to be a constructive push,
"the positive move that moral/spiritual resources can be experienced as
purely immanent. . . . We need to see how it became possible to experience moral fullness, to identify the locus of our highest moral capacity
and inspiration, without reference to God, but within the range of purely
intra-human powers" (pp. 244-45).[9] It is the order of mutual benefit that

9. Taylor's notion of "fullness" has been a matter of critique. See, for example, Jonathan
Sheehan, "When Was Disenchantment? History and the Secular Age," in *Varieties of Secu-
larism in a Secular Age,* ed. Michael Warner, Jonathan VanAntwerpen, and Craig Calhoun
(Cambridge: Harvard University Press, 2010), pp. 217-42, at 229-31. The critique is generally

provides this mechanism. The order of mutual benefit offered a moral goal that was experienced as an obligation but was at the same time achievable — and achievable under our own steam, so to speak.

Here Taylor the Hegelian argues that, even though it rejects Christianity, exclusive humanism was only possible having come *through* Christianity. The order of mutual benefit is a kind of secularization of Christian universalism — the call to love the neighbor, even the enemy. If Christianity renounced the tribalisms of paganism, exclusive humanism's vision of mutual benefit takes that universalizing impulse but now arrogates it to a self-sufficient human capability. We *ought* to be concerned with others, we *ought* to be altruistic, and *we* have the capacity to achieve this ideal. Thus, once again, Taylor describes this as an "immanentizing move": "the main thrust of modern exclusive humanism has tried . . . to immanentize this capacity of beneficence." We need to appreciate "the way in which modern humanisms innovated in relation to the ancients, drawing on the forms of Christian faith they emerged from: active re-ordering; instrumental rationality; universalism; benevolence. But of course their aim was also to reject the Christian aspiration to transcend flourishing. Hence only the self-giving which conduced to general flourishing as now defined was allowed as rational and natural, and even that within reasonable bounds. The rest was condemned as extravagance, or 'enthusiasm'" (p. 247). What exclusive humanism devotes itself to as the "moral fullness" possible within immanence will turn out to be an "agape-analogue" that is

---

that the category of "fullness" smuggles in a specific religious notion under the guise of a general or universal concept. In his afterword, Taylor clarifies his intention, without backing away from the universalism of his claim: "I wanted to use this as something like a category term to capture the very different ways in which each of us (as I claim) sees life as capable of some fuller, higher, more genuine, more authentic, more intense . . . form. The list of adjectives is indefinitely long, because the positions we may adopt have no finite limit. Why do this? Because I think that it is valuable to try to grasp a position you find unfamiliar and even baffling through trying to bring into focus the understanding of fullness that it involves. This is particularly the case if you want really to understand it, to be able to feel the power it has for its protagonists, as against simply dismissing it" (*Secular Age*, p. 315). To get a sense of what phenomenon Taylor is trying to name, consider Hubert Dreyfus and Sean Dorrance Kelly's notion of the "whoosh," a "wave" that overwhelms (*All Things Shining: Reading the Western Classics to Find Meaning in a Secular Age* [New York: Free Press, 2011], pp. 199-202).

dependent on Christianity.[10] Indeed, Taylor's (rather Hegelian) claim is quite strong: "it would probably not have been possible to make the transition to exclusive humanism on any other basis" (p. 247).[11]

"So exclusive humanism wasn't just something we fell into, once the old myths dissolved or the 'infamous' ancien régime church was crushed" (p. 255). Exclusive humanism is an *achievement:* "the development of this purely immanent sense of universal solidarity is an important achievement, a milestone in human history" (p. 255). Indeed, discovering immanent resources for fullness and meaning in this way will become "the charter of modern unbelief" (p. 257).

Religion for Moderns

The anthropocentric shifts we've just noted find mirror images in shifts in religion itself. In chapter 7, Taylor tracks this corresponding "change in the understanding of God." Once again, Taylor is interested in the ways that, in the Latin West, Christianity was both an unwitting progenitor *and a reflector* of the new modern social imaginary, even as it was trying to resist it.

What becomes increasingly distasteful (the word is chosen advisedly) is the notion of God's *agency,* and hence the personhood of God. Sometimes dismissed as a feature of gauche "enthusiasm," at other times seen as a threat to an ordered cosmos, there would be an increasing interest in jettisoning the notion of "God as an agent intervening in history. He could be agent qua original Architect of the universe, but not as the author of myriad particular interventions, 'miraculous' or not, which were the stuff of popular piety and orthodox religion" (p. 275). Such an active God would violate the buffer zone we have created to protect ourselves from such incursions. And so the "god" that governs the cosmos is the architect of an *im*personal order. In short, we're all Masons now.

But to reject God's personhood and agency entailed rejecting an en-

10. The agape-analogue, of course, is very different from Christian agape precisely because of its immanentization and hence refusal of *grace.* This is why it must reflect "an activist, interventionist stance, both towards nature and to human society" (*Secular Age,* p. 246).

11. And "the transition didn't have to happen," he adds (p. 248).

tire fabric of Christianity that revolved around the notion of religion as *communion*.[12] According to historic, orthodox Christian faith, "salvation is thwarted to the extent that we treat God as an impersonal being, or as merely the creator of an impersonal order to which we have to adjust. Salvation is only effected by, one might say, our being in communion with God through the community of humans in communion, viz., the church" (pp. 278-79). To depersonalize God is to deny the importance of communion and the community *of* communion that is the church, home to that meal that is called "Communion."

So it is not surprising, then, that the "religion" of this impersonal order is also de-Communion-ed, de-ritualized, and disembodied. Taylor helpfully describes this as a process of **excarnation**. In contrast to the central conviction of Christian faith — that the transcendent God became *in*carnate, en-fleshed, in Jesus of Nazareth — *ex*carnation is a move of disembodiment and abstraction, an aversion of and flight from the particularities of embodiment (and communion). This will be a "purified" religion — purified of rituals and relics, but also of emotion and bodies (p. 288) — of which Kant's "rational" religion is the apotheosis. With the body goes the Body; that is, with the abandonment of material religion we see the diminishment of the church as a communion as well. The "Deist standpoint involves disintricating the issue of religious truth from participation in a certain community practice of religious life, into which facets of prayer, faith, hope are woven" (p. 293).

We might describe this as "deistic" religion — if it didn't look like so much contemporary Protestantism.[13] And we might be tempted to identify this with the "liberal" streams of Protestantism — if it didn't sound like so many "progressive" evangelicals. Taylor sees this as an open door

12. Taylor sees Christianity summed up in the theme of communion: "the central concept which makes sense of the whole is communion, or love, defining both the nature of God, and our relation to him" (p. 279).

13. Taylor is quite unapologetic about this later in the book when he claims that "the direction of this Reform was towards a far-reaching excarnation" (p. 614) and that "the development of Reformed Christianity . . . worked to sideline the body" (p. 611). Indeed, he says this is "one of the main contentions of this book" (p. 614). However, this should be tempered if we note — however ad hoc — an increased attention to embodiment, ritual, and the aesthetic amongst Protestant evangelicals.

for exclusive humanism and atheism; it is a pretty straight line from excarnation to the vilification of religion (pp. 293-94) — which raises important questions for Christianity in the new millennium.

But let's keep this in mind: to this point, Taylor has only got us to something like the seventeenth century! There's a lot of the story to come. But in closing part 2, Taylor offers a helpful summary of his analysis and argument thus far:

> So putting this all together, we can see how a certain kind of framework understanding came to be constituted: fed by the powerful presence of impersonal orders, cosmic, social, and moral; drawn by the power of the disengaged stance, and its ethical prestige, and ratified by a sense of what the alternative was, based on an élite's derogatory and somewhat fearful portrait of popular religion, an unshakeable sense could arise of our inhabiting an immanent, impersonal order, which screened out, for those who inhabited it, all phenomena which failed to fit this framework. (p. 288)

Taylor's earlier criticism of Protestant "disenchantment" finds a corollary in this loss of communion, and hence the loss of the Eucharist as central to the practice of Christian worship. **Could we imagine a Protestantism that has room for both Word *and* Table — for that "faith that comes by hearing" *and* communion with the triune God?** One might suggest that this is just the Protestantism found in John Calvin, despite the flattened spirituality of his professed heirs.

It turns out it's not so hard to see ourselves four hundred years ago; it's as if we're looking at childhood photos of our contemporary culture.

CHAPTER 3

The Malaise of Immanence: The "Feel" of a Secular Age

Part 1 of *A Secular Age* ("The Work of Reform") considered the late medieval and early modern reform movements that began to shift the plausibility conditions of the West, making exclusive humanism a possibility (especially via disenchantment and the newly buffered self). But this was only a condition of possibility, not inevitability. Part 2 ("The Turning Point") considered the positive shift that really made exclusive humanism a "live option": a theological shift that gave us the impersonal god of deism coupled with the intellectual and cultural Pelagianism that found the resources for an "agape-analogue" within immanence. This gave us a way to be rid of eternity and transcendence without giving up a "moral project" — a vision and task that give significance to our striving.

What this means, of course, is that Taylor has now brought us to a secular$_3$ age — an age in which the plausibility structures have changed, the conditions of belief have shifted, and theistic belief is not only displaced from being the default, it is positively *contested*. We're not in Christendom anymore.

In part 3 of his analysis and argument ("The Nova Effect"), Taylor — while still in a historical mode — is starting to give us a sense of the existential "feel" of what it means to inhabit these new "conditions of belief." In short, he's beginning to try to capture what it *feels* like to live in a secular$_3$ age.[1] Far

1. Recall Colin Jager's helpful insight into how the argument of *A Secular Age* works:

from being a monolithic space or "experience," our secular age is marked by tensions and fractures. While exclusive humanism becomes a live option, it doesn't immediately capture everyone's imagination. Indeed, the backlash begins almost immediately. So the space of our secular age is fraught, and in part 3 Taylor is in the mode of a cultural anthropologist trying to capture just how and why this is the case. In this respect, he is a more reliable guide to our present than those confident secularists$_2$ who would lead us to believe that a "secular" world is a cool, monolithic, "rational" age where everyone who's anyone (i.e., smart people who are not religious) lives in quiet confidence.[2]

....
Born with a reason,
blown out like a ghost.
We came with our best lines,
told them like jokes.
If I could have known then
we were dying to get gone . . .
I can't believe we get just one.

Blind Pilot, "Just One"
We Are the Tide (2011)

Taylor doesn't buy it. On his account, our secular age is haunted, and always has been. Certainly belief is contested and contestable in our secular age. There's no going back. Even seeking enchantment will always and only be reenchantment *after* disenchantment.[3] But almost as soon as unbelief becomes an option, unbelievers begin to have doubts — which is to say, they begin to wonder if there isn't something "more." They worry about the shape of a world so flattened by disenchantment. In part 3 (summarized in this chapter), Taylor paints a picture of the fraught

"Taylor's question — namely, 'What does secularity feel like from the inside?' — is the sort of question that can be asked only *after* a certain kind of secular age" (Colin Jager, "This Detail, This History: Charles Taylor's Romanticism," in *Varieties of Secularism in a Secular Age*, ed. Michael Warner, Jonathan VanAntwerpen, and Craig Calhoun [Cambridge: Harvard University Press, 2010], p. 173).

2. In other words: the world painted in the novels of Ian McEwan and Martin Amis (in contrast, say, to the novelistic worlds of Julian Barnes and David Foster Wallace).

3. Elsewhere Taylor emphasizes that "the process of disenchantment is irreversible. The aspiration to reenchant . . . points to a different process, which may indeed reproduce features analogous to the enchanted world, but does not in any simple sense restore it." See Taylor, "Disenchantment-Reenchantment," in *Dilemmas and Connections: Selected Essays* (Cambridge: Harvard University Press, Belknap Press, 2011), p. 287.

dynamics of a secular age that have enduring significance for understanding our present.

The Nova Effect: Fragilization from Cross-Pressures

The outcome of the turn documented in part 2 is what Taylor calls the "**nova effect**." The astronomical metaphor indicates an explosion of options for finding (or creating) "significance." The cross-polemics that result from new options for belief and unbelief "end up generating a number of new positions . . . so that our present predicament offers a gamut of possible positions." We find ourselves caught between myriad options for pursuing meaning, significance, and fullness. The "nova effect" names this fragmentation (p. 299), pluralization (p. 300), and **fragilization** (p. 304) of our visions of the good life and human flourishing: pluralized because of the sheer array of options; fragilized because of proximity and frequency. As Taylor observes, there is something different about this plurality in a secular age:

> This kind of multiplicity of faiths has little effect as long as it is neutralized by the sense that being like them is not really an option for me. As long as the alternative is strange and other, perhaps despised, but perhaps just too different, too weird, too incomprehensible, so that becoming *that* isn't really conceivable for me, so long will their difference not undermine my embedding in my own faith. This changes when through increased contact, interchange, even perhaps inter-marriage, the other becomes more and more like me, in everything else but faith: same activities, professions, opinions, tastes, etc. Then the issue posed by the difference becomes more insistent: why my way, and not hers? There is no other difference left to make the shift preposterous or unimaginable. (p. 304)

Ironically, it is the overwhelming homogeneity of our lives in modernity that makes our faith stances all that more strange and contested: "Homogeneity and instability work together to bring the fragilizing effect of pluralism to a maximum" (p. 304).

The result is a "nova" effect because this produces not just a binary choice between two options but an array of options that almost metastasize because of the multiple "cross-pressures" of this pluralized situation (p. 302). This is why "we are now living in a spiritual super-nova, a kind of galloping pluralism on the spiritual plane" (p. 300).

Taylor's analysis of this point is deeply existential. As he puts it, while the world is disenchanted for "us moderns," we nonetheless also experience a sense of *loss* and *malaise* in the wake of such disenchantment (p. 302). As I noted in the introduction, I think one can feel such cross-pressures in the fiction of David Foster Wallace. One might feel something similar in the poetry of Mary Oliver — whose popularity probably owes less to the intrinsic merit of her poetry and more to her ability to give voice to this feeling of cross-pressure shared by so many. All sorts of people feel themselves caught in these "cross-pressures" — pushed by the immanence of disenchantment on one side, but also pushed by a sense of significance and transcendence on another side, even if it might be a lost transcendence.

Note how much Taylor's account here relies on an appeal to a "sense" that "we" have, a "feel" for this. "My point," he emphasizes, "is not that

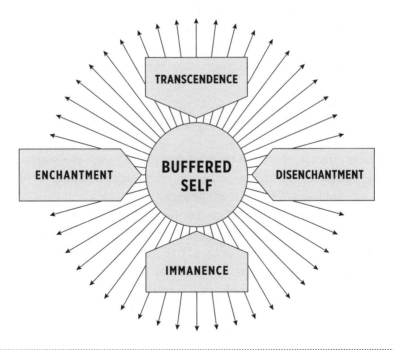

Figure 1. Nova effect from cross-pressures in a secular$_3$ age.

everybody feels this, but rather, first, that many people do, and far beyond the ranks of card-carrying theists." All sorts of people feel themselves caught; "in the face of the opposition between orthodoxy and unbelief, many, and among them the best and most sensitive minds, were [and are] cross-pressured, looking for a third way" (p. 302). It is the intensity of these cross-pressures that causes the explosion, the nova effect, which is effectively an explosion of all sorts of "third ways."

But what attends this explosion is also a malaise that is itself one of the consequences of a buffered identity. The same "buffering" of the self that protects us also encloses us and isolates us. "This malaise is specific to a buffered identity, whose very invulnerability opens it to the danger that not just evil spirits, cosmic forces or gods won't 'get to' it, but that nothing significant will stand out for us" (p. 303). Sealed off from enchantment, the modern buffered self is also sealed off from significance, left to ruminate in a stew of its own ennui. It is just this sealing off that generates the pressure: the self's "relative invulnerability to anything beyond the human world" also leads to "a sense that something may be occluded in the very closure which guarantees safety" (p. 303). Our insulation breeds a sense of cosmic isolation. We might have underestimated the ability of disenchantment to sustain significance. But now there's no going back.

Reactions: The Malaises of Immanence

The nova effect is, in important ways, generated by the cross-pressures on the buffered self. However, other causal factors contribute to this supernova explosion of immanent spiritualities in our secular age. There emerges a kind of "package" of modernity; the "whole package" includes "buffered identity, with its disengaged subjectivity, with its supporting disciplines, all sustaining an order of freedom and mutual benefit" (pp. 304-5). Pluralization is generated in no small part by negative reactions to this modern package as a whole, or at least different aspects of the package. "We moderns" are not entirely comfortable with modernity. These negative reactions include Romanticism and Pietism, which contribute to some of the options exploding out of the cross-pressured situation. In other words, Romanticism and Pietism are part of the nova effect.

But there are negative reactions to orthodox Christianity as well — "indictments against orthodox religion." Once again, a central part of this indictment is fueled by theodicy, or lack thereof (p. 305; cp. 232). In other words, we now have the rise of the evidential argument from evil: if God is all-good and all-powerful, then there shouldn't be evil. But there is evil. Therefore, *this* God must not exist.

This sort of skeptical argument could only take hold within the modern moral order (MMO) and its epistemic confidence: "Once we claim to understand the universe, and how it works; once we even try to explain how it works by invoking its being created for our benefit, then this explanation is open to clear challenge: we know how things go, and we know why they were set up, and we can judge whether the first meets the purpose defined in the second. In Lisbon 1755, it seems clearly not to have. So the immanent order ups the ante" (p. 306).[4] But we have to appreciate what has changed here: precisely the emergence of the disengaged, "world picture" confidence in our powers of exhaustive surveillance (cp. p. 232). Prior to this stance, the conditions would have yielded lament, not theodicy: "If one is in a profoundly believing/practicing way of life, then this hanging in to trust in God may seem the obvious way, and is made easier by the fact that everyone is with you in this" (p. 306).

Taylor then returns to consider the negative reactions to disenchantment and the buffered self — recalling that these reactions increase the pressure in the "cross-pressures." While he's going to provide a taxonomy of these different sorts of reactions, he suggests that all of them hinge on a common "axis": the "generalized sense in our culture that with the eclipse of the transcendent, *something may have been lost*" (p. 307, emphasis added; the optative mood is intentional). It is this lack, loss, and emptiness that — in and by the absence of transcendence — *press* on the immanence of exclusive humanism, yielding what Taylor calls "the malaises of immanence" (p. 309). The new epistemic expectation that comes with enclosure in immanence — namely, that whatever is within the sphere of immanence should be understandable to us — means we expect an *answer* to such mat-

4. The Lisbon earthquake of 1755 generated an array of responses to the "problem of evil," most notably from Leibniz. For further discussion, see Susan Neiman's important book *Evil in Modern Thought: An Alternative History of Philosophy* (Princeton: Princeton University Press, 2002). My thanks to Chris Ganski for this reference.

ters. Inscrutability is no longer an option; so if believers have no rationally demonstrative answer, but can only appeal to something like the "hidden" will of God, then the scales tip in favor of what *we* know and understand.

This epistemic expectation gives rise to an existential permission: we can rebel and revolt. "The failure of theodicy can now more readily lead to rebellion, because of our heightened sense of ourselves as free agents" (p. 306). And in the face of evil, we can even begin to find a strange comfort in being alone, without God or the gods: "There is a kind of peace in being on my/our (human) own, in solidarity against the blind universe which wrought this horror." But this is a possibility "opened by the modern sense of immanent order" (p. 306).

But if there are continued reactions against faith, particularly orthodox Christianity — think of these as options that push back on the vertical pressure of transcendence and the horizontal pressure of enchantment — we can't ignore other reactions that push back against the suffocation of immanence and the hegemony of disenchantment. Taylor emphasizes that this latter "axis" of reaction is more familiar than we might admit (especially if "we" are intellectual elites). "There is a generalized sense in our culture," he claims, "that with the eclipse of the transcendent, something may have been lost."[5] Recall Julian Barnes's plaintive quip: "I don't believe in God, but I miss Him." Or consider the lyrics of the song playing in this coffee shop as I write this:

I was raised up believing
I was somehow unique
Like a snowflake, distinct among snowflakes,
Unique in each way you can see.
And, now, after some thinking, I'd say I'd rather be

---

5. Taylor tries to qualify the claim: "I put it in the optative mood, because people react very differently to this; some endorse this idea of loss, and seek to define what it is. Others want to downplay it, and paint it as an optional reaction, something we are in for only as long as we allow ourselves to wallow in nostalgia. Still others again, while standing as firmly on the side of disenchantment as the critics of nostalgia, nevertheless accept that this sense of loss is inevitable; it is the price we pay for modernity and rationality, but we must courageously accept this bargain, and lucidly opt for what we have inevitably become" (p. 307). He identifies this last response with Max Weber.

A functioning cog in some great machinery,
Serving something beyond me.

But I don't, I don't know what that will be.
I'll get back to you someday soon, you will see.

What's my name; what's my station?
Oh, just tell me what I should do.[6]

What's at work here? Taylor describes it in terms of a vague sense of loss or lack: "our actions, goals, achievements, and the like, have a lack of weight, gravity, thickness, substance. There is a deeper resonance which they lack, which we feel should be there" (p. 307). This "felt flatness" can manifest itself in different ways at different times. For example, it can be felt with particular force in rites of passage in life: birth, marriage, death. We continue to feel a pressure and need to mark it somehow. "The way we have always done this is by linking these moments up with the transcendent, the highest, the holy, the sacred. Pre-Axial religions did this. But the enclosure in the immanent leaves a hole here. Many people, who have no other connection or felt affinity with religion, go on using the ritual of the church for these rites de passage" (p. 309).

One can feel something like this in David Rieff's memoir of the final illness and death of his mother, Susan Sontag. On the one hand, Rieff is ruthlessly "rational" about the experience; even if his mother was tempted by faiths of various sorts, Rieff won't take any "consolation in unreason."[7] But on the other hand, his questions attest to some sort of cross-pressure. "Am I to ascribe some special meaning to the intensity of her final years, as if somehow she had a premonition that her time was ending?" he asks. "Or is all of this just that vain, irrational human wish to ascribe meaning when no meaning is really on offer?"[8] It's not that he's tempted by faith or toying with reenchantment; it's that ruthless disenchantment seems more than we can bear. And so Rieff takes us with him

6. Fleet Foxes, "Helplessness Blues." Cp. also Arcade Fire, *The Suburbs*.

7. David Rieff, *Swimming in a Sea of Death: A Son's Memoir* (New York: Simon and Schuster, 2008), p. 78.

8. Rieff, *Swimming in a Sea,* pp. 18-19.

on his last trip to Paris with his mother: "me in my window seat . . . she in the hold," en route to be buried in Montparnasse, "the most literary of cemeteries, a veritable Parnassus." "Except, of course, that it's nothing of the sort — not unless you believe in spirits or the Christian fairy tale of resurrection, anyway — and for a simple reason: the men and women in question no longer exist. The best one can do, and I'm not sure I believe a word of it, is say along with Bei Dao that 'as long as one's thoughts are spoken and written down, they'll form another life, they won't perish with the flesh.' "[9] Well, yes, one could at least say that — because what would be the other option? And so we see Rieff at the cemetery. The unsentimental son is not without his rituals: "And so it ended. As her corpse was lowered into the grave, and I knelt at the edge of the burial hole, I felt she was still there. Today, when I go to visit my mother's grave, I do not know what to do besides tidy up a bit (me tidying up for my mother! — a preposterous reversal of roles). In any case, the cemetery gardeners do an excellent job, as do the many visitors to the gravesite. But I do not believe she is there, or anywhere else of course, and so I rarely stay long." And yet he goes. "I arrive, walking quickly past Beauvoir, past Beckett. And once I've arrived I stare for a few moments. Then I kneel, kiss the granite slab, and get back up on my feet. And then I go — hurriedly, confusedly — past Beckett and Beauvoir again if I retrace my steps, and past Cioran if I do not. It is not just that I have nothing intelligent to say: I am incapable of thought."[10] As Cormac McCarthy's narrator says in *The Road*, "Where you've nothing else construct ceremonies out of the air and breathe upon them." It's a way to deal with the pressure of the loss.

Recall the shape of Taylor's account here: the feeling of *loss* exerts its own kind of *pressure,* the strange pressure of an absence. And if that can be felt in the momentous, it can also be felt in the mundane. Indeed, "this can be where it most hurts," he concedes: "some people feel a terrible flatness in the everyday, and this experience has been identified particularly with commercial, industrial, or consumer society. They feel emptiness of the repeated, accelerating cycle of desire and fulfillment, in consumer culture; the cardboard quality of bright supermarkets, or

9. Rieff, *Swimming in a Sea*, pp. 175, 172.
10. Rieff, *Swimming in a Sea*, pp. 176-77.

neat row housing in a clean suburb" (p. 309).[11] Material abundance can engender this existential sense of lack precisely because the swelling of immanence seems unable to make up for a pressure we still feel — from transcendence, from enchantment.

This analysis of "loss" is an example of Taylor in his phenomenological mode, trying to identify and name a feature of what he takes to be a common experience for those who inhabit a secular$_3$ age. His claim is forthright, but qualified: "wherever people stand on this issue, everyone understands, or *feels* they understand what is being talked about here. This is a *sense* which, at least in its optative form, seems available to everyone, whatever interpretation they end up putting on it" (p. 307, emphasis added). Note his appeal to a *sense:* this is an analysis you'll find convincing if his phenomenology has just named something that's been haunting you. If not, then Taylor doesn't have any "proof" to offer you.[12]

The loss creates a pressure. Now, as he rightly notes, "it doesn't follow that the only cure for [it] is a return to transcendence" (p. 309). The dissatisfaction and emptiness *can* propel a return to transcendence. But often — and perhaps more often than not now? — the "cure" to this nagging pressure of absence is sought *within immanence,* and it is this quest that generates the nova effect, looking for love/meaning/significance/quasi "transcendence" *within* the immanent order.[13] "[These seekers] too seek solutions, or ways of filling the lack, but within immanence; and thus the gamut of new positions multiplies" (p. 310) — hence supernova.

---

11. Arcade Fire's 2010 album *The Suburbs* is a veritable sound track of just this malaise.

12. As he admits, "This is just an attempt to give some shape to a general malaise, and I recognize how questionable it is, and how many other descriptions could have been offered here" (pp. 307-8).

13. One could, of course, run an entire Augustinian analysis of this as the doomed project of loving some part of creation *instead of* the Creator (à la book 4 of the *Confessions* and passim). But Taylor doesn't invoke "idolatry" as a conceptual frame here, for obvious strategic reasons.

An Imaginary-Shift: The Modern Cosmic Imaginary

Taylor's story then leaps ahead; we are now plunked into the nineteenth century, famous for an explosion of unbelief.[14] But Taylor suggests that the unbelief of the nineteenth century is *not* just more of the same, the growth and steady accumulation of the nova effect. No, he argues, "the turn to unbelief in the middle or later nineteenth century is in a way something new. . . . It is in a sense deeper" (p. 322). Why? Because it now reflects a shift in our *modern COSMIC imaginary* — the "shift from cosmos to universe" has now started to take root in our social imaginary: "social" in the sense of being shared by many, not just intellectuals and elites; "imaginary" because it isn't just a theory or metaphysic held by a few elite intellectuals but is more like the worldview that more and more people take for granted as "the way things are." In other words, there has now been a fundamental shift in how people *imagine* nature, their environment, and our cosmic context. "I want to emphasize that I am talking about our *sense* of things. I'm not talking about what people believe. Many still hold that the universe is created by God, that in some sense it is governed by his Providence. What I am talking about is the way the universe is spontaneously imagined, and therefore experienced" (p. 325). This is not about "how one *theory* displaced another," Taylor emphasizes. When the story is confined to that theoretical level, it's told as a subtraction story. But Taylor emphasizes that we're not primarily talking about a change in *theory,* because most people don't theorize! However, we all do "spontaneously imagine" ourselves in a cosmic context, and it's *that* which Taylor is after: "I'm interested," he says, in "how our *sense* of things, our cosmic imaginary, in other words, our whole background understanding and *feel* of the world has been transformed" (p. 325, emphasis added).[15]

Taylor encapsulates this imaginary-shift as the move from a "cosmos"

14. See, for example, David Hempton, *Evangelical Disenchantment: Nine Portraits of Faith and Doubt* (New Haven: Yale University Press, 2008), and Timothy Larsen, *Crisis of Doubt: Honest Faith in Nineteenth-Century England* (New York: Oxford University Press, 2009).

15. This is not so far away from Thomas Kuhn's notion of a "paradigm," which is also a background set of assumptions of what is taken for granted and thus *not* articulated or

to a "universe" — the move of spontaneously imagining our cosmic environment as an ordered, layered, hierarchical, shepherded *place* to spontaneously imagining our cosmic environment as an infinite, cavernous, anonymous *space*. While this shift might have been prompted and amplified by increasing empirical evidence (geological evidence pointing to an older earth; astronomical evidence pointing to an expanding universe; etc.), Taylor emphasizes the *existential* nature of this shift. First, there is a fundamental *extension* of the cosmic environment — in space and time — that is uncanny, *Unheimlich,* dis-placing, such that we no longer feel that we "fit" into a cosmos as a cosmic home. Instead we see ourselves adrift and cast into an anonymous, cold "universe": "Reality in all directions plunges its roots into the unknown and as yet unmappable. It is this sense which defines the grasp of the world as 'universe' and not 'cosmos'; and this is what I mean when I say that the universe outlook was 'deep' in a way the cosmos picture was not" (p. 326). And so we find ourselves now in the "dark abyss of time": "Humans are no longer charter members of the cosmos, but occupy merely a narrow band of recent time," for example (p. 327).

Second, there is the increasing sense that things *evolve* (p. 327) — a sense that precedes Darwin. In such a picture we lose the cosmos's forms and essences — the order created by design. This might also explain the new design-fixation as a response in this era (the sort that generates Paley's famous design argument for the existence of God): "What makes for the heat at this neuralgic point is that there is a strong sense of deficit in a world where people used to feel a presence here, and were accustomed to this support; often couldn't help feeling the lack of this support as undermining their whole faith; and very much needed to be reassured that it oughtn't to" (p. 329). Such design fixation is also already a sign of waning devotional practice: "once people come to live more and more in purely secular time, when God's eternity and the attendant span of creation becomes merely a *belief,* however well backed up with reasons, the imagination can easily be nudged towards other ways of accounting for the awkward facts" (p. 328).

---

made explicit. Hence this section is entitled "imaginary-shift" to play on Kuhn's notion of a "paradigm shift."

What's the result of such a shift? Well, even believers end up defending a theistic *universe* rather than the biblical *cosmos*. Eliminating mystery as a consequence of Protestant critiques of allegorization (p. 330),[16] even believers end up reading the Bible as if it were a treatise on such a universe; in short, you get the emergence of young earth creationism (p. 330). Indeed, we only get the so-called war between science and religion once the modern cosmic imaginary has seeped into both believers and unbelievers; at that point, "these defenders of the faith share a temper with its most implacable enemies" (p. 331). In other words, no one is more modern than a fundamentalist. This is why the "face-off between 'religion' and 'science'" has a "strangely intra-mural quality" (p. 331). But this supposed "pure face-off between 'religion' and 'science' is a chimaera, or rather, an ideological construct. In reality, there is a struggle between thinkers with complex, many-levelled agendas" (p. 332).[17]

One can understand the trajectory that leads from this cosmic imaginary to materialism; if the immanent is going to be self-sufficient, as it were, then the material has to be all there is. The straightforwardness of

16. On this point, cp. the important history by Peter Harrison, *The Bible, Protestantism, and the Rise of Natural Science* (Cambridge: Cambridge University Press, 2001).

17. Taylor considers Thomas Burnet and Vico as "key figures in the transition of the cosmic imaginary" because in them we can see "how what we now see as a modern cosmic imaginary is beginning to shape their religious outlook and sensibility" (p. 333). Or as he'll put it elsewhere, we'll see that nature now figures in their *ethical* and *aesthetic* imaginations in a new way (pp. 347ff.). The picture — the "imaginary" — of this new "universe" has several different elements: a sense of living in the ruins of a "deep time," the rise of a sense of the "sublime," and an increasing sense of the "dark genesis of humanity" (p. 335). Taylor focuses on the sense of the sublime as a kind of "case study" in nova-effect meaning-generation — an example of how the new cosmic imaginary called forth a kind of transcendence-substitute. The sublime is generated by what Burnet describes as "Excess," aroused by "the boundlessness of the heavens, or by high mountains, vast oceans, trackless deserts" (p. 335). The sublime then becomes a mode of something like immanent (quasi) transcendence. "We need to have our petty circle of life broken open. The membrane of self-absorption has to be broken from the outside" — and the sublime fits the bill without introducing all the problems of transcendence "proper." "The sight of 'Excess,' vast, strange, unencompassable, provoking fear, even horror, breaks through this self-absorption and awakens our sense of what is really important, whether this be the infinity of God, as with Burnet, our supersensible moral vocation, as with Kant; or, as with later thinkers, our capacity for heroic affirmation of meaning in the face of the world without telos — the truth of eternal recurrence" (p. 339).

that trajectory is recognized by Taylor, but holds little interest for him. Instead, he is interested in another trajectory embedded in this imaginary-shift; there is an enduring "sense of our deep nature, of a current running through all things, which also resonates in us; the experience of being opened up to something deeper and fuller by contact with Nature; the sense of an intra-cosmic mystery, which was quite missing from Providential Deism" (p. 350). In other words, some of the "nova" reactions to cross-pressure generate a new sense of the charmed, charged nature of our being-in-the-world. "Some people may even want to claim that we cannot make sense of them within a totally materialist outlook" — and recent books by Dreyfus, Kelly, and Thomas Nagel attest to this. The "salient feature of the modern cosmic imaginary" that Taylor highlights "is that it has opened a space in which people can wander between and around all these options without having to land clearly and definitely in any one. In the wars between belief and unbelief, this can be seen as a kind of no-man's-land; except that it has got wide enough to take on the character of a neutral zone, where one can escape the war altogether. Indeed, this is part of the reason why the war is constantly running out of steam in modern civilization, in spite of the efforts of zealous minorities" (p. 351). Those minorities are fundamentalists of various stripes — whether religious or new atheist — who fail to recognize the cross-pressured space we inhabit.

Expanding Unbelief

Borrowed Capital from Transcendence

So we live in cross-pressured space, the space of the nova effect, plural and complicated — unlike the supposedly secure and dogmatic zones one would expect if one believed the so-called war between belief and unbelief. Most of us, Taylor argues, do not live in the confident camps of such a war; rather, most of us live in this cross-pressured no-man's-land between them.

What is unique in Taylor's story is the significance he accords to both the Renaissance and Romanticism. Philosophical accounts of modernity

— and hence our present (or "postmodernity") — tend to have an epistemological fixation that seizes upon the Enlightenment as the center of the story.[18] But Taylor's account is much more nuanced, recognizing early and important shifts in the Renaissance. Even more importantly, Taylor accords a central role to Romanticism as a turning point — a kind of countermodernity within modernity. This is why "we can see the Victorians as our contemporaries in a way which we cannot easily extend to the men of the Enlightenment" (p. 369).

Hence in chapter 10, in contrast to the subtraction stories that focus on scientific enlightenment, Taylor considers the central role of *art* in creating this "open space" that characterizes our secular age. One of the features of post-Romantic art, he suggests, is a fundamental shift from art as *mimesis* to art as *poeisis* — from art *imitating* nature to art *making* its world. This was necessary precisely because the flattening of the world meant the loss of reference. We find ourselves in Baudelaire's "forest of symbols" but without tether or hook, without any *given* to which the symbols/signs refer. Enclosed in the immanent frame, which is now the home of the buffered self, the best we can do is "triangulate" meaning from our signs, through historical nostalgia, to our present (pp. 352-53). So, in poetry, for instance, "where formerly poetic language could rely on certain publicly available orders of meaning, it now has to consist in a language of articulated sensibility." The "poet must articulate his own world of references"; in other words, the poet has to create a/the world. Taylor sees similar shifts in painting and music (pp. 353-54).[19]

Taylor describes this as yet another "disembedding" by which art now begins to emerge as an autonomous entity and institution. In earlier societies, the aesthetic was embroiled with the religious and the political — what we look back on as ancient "art objects" were, in fact and function, *liturgical* instruments, etc. What we see in modernity, however, is a shift whereby the aesthetic aspect is distilled and disclosed for its own sake and as the object of interest. And from this emerges "art" as a cultural

18. For a helpful exception, see Peter Leithart, *Solomon among the Postmoderns* (Grand Rapids: Brazos, 2007).

19. For a rich engagement with the history of music in modernity in light of Taylor's argument, see Jeremy Begbie, *Music, Modernity, and God* (Cambridge: Cambridge University Press, 2014).

phenomenon and an autonomous reality (p. 355). So now we go to hear Bach's *Mass in B Minor* (a liturgical work whose "home," as it were, is in worship) in a concert hall to "appreciate" it as a work of art disembedded from that liturgical home. This is a "desemanticisation and resemanticisation" whereby the art is decontextualized from its religious origins and then recontextualized *as* "art."[20]

Thus Taylor sees the emergence of "absolute music" as the culmination of this disembedding (ab-solute in the sense of music that is ab-solved of connection to such contexts). Whereas the music that accompanied the Mass or even the play was tethered to action and a story, engendering responses within a community of practice that knew the references, "with the new music, we have the response in some way captured, made real, there unfolding before us; but the object isn't there. The music moves us very strongly, because it is moved, as it were; it captures, expresses, incarnates being profoundly moved. (Think of Beethoven quartets.) But what at? What is the object? Is there an object?" (p. 355). Nevertheless, we can't quite shake our feeling that "there must be an object." And so, Taylor suggests, even this disembedded art "trades on resonances of the cosmic in us" (p. 356). And conveniently, art is never going to ask of you anything you wouldn't want to do. So we get significance without any ascetic moral burden.

But how does this create the "open space" of the nova effect? In what way do these artistic shifts make room for cross-pressured options and alternatives? Well, these "subtler languages operating in the 'absolute' mode can offer a place to go for modern unbelief"; more specifically, they provide an outlet and breathing room for those who feel cross-pressured precisely by the Romantic critique of the deism and anthropocentric shifts that have flattened the world, leaving no room for mystery. For those who can't tolerate such ruthless flattening of instrumental reason (and Taylor thinks our better nature will never tolerate that), this emergence of the arts provides another venue for a kind of immanent *mystery,* an anthropologized mystery within.[21] The arts and the aesthetic become

20. Recall Julian Barnes's recognition of this (noted in the introduction), and his musing whether actually *believing* would make a difference for how the work is appreciated.

21. Cp. Rorty on the new role of art in *Philosophy and the Mirror of Nature,* thirtieth anniversary ed. (Princeton: Princeton University Press, 2009), pp. 4-5.

a way of working out "the feeling that there is something inadequate in our way of life, that we live by an order which represses what is really important" (p. 358, focusing on Schiller, *Letters on the Aesthetic Education of Man*). The result is an immanent space to try to satisfy a lost longing for transcendence; in short, this creates a "place to go for modern unbelief" without having to settle for the utterly flattened world of mechanism or utilitarianism — but also without having to return to religion proper. And so we get the new sacred spaces of modernity: the concert hall as temple; the museum as chapel; tourism as the new pilgrimage (p. 360).

It's worth noting the ambiguity of Taylor's reading here: on the one hand, this impulse could simply come from an older longing that we've outgrown — a *historical* pressure (p. 361); on the other hand, he sometimes seems to suggest that this pressure comes from the now-ignored transcendent *itself,* "the solicitations of the spiritual" (p. 360). On the one hand, one might simply claim that we're still haunted because we're still too close to the time when we *used to* believe in ghosts; on the other hand (and one gets the sense this is Taylor's position), we might be haunted because, well, there's a Ghost there. (To paraphrase Kurt Cobain: just because you're paranoid doesn't mean they're not after you.) Who's to adjudicate between these two options? From where? Aware of that ambiguity, Taylor's phenomenology speaks into that contested space and simply says, "Try this account on for size. Does it make sense of something you've *felt?*"

Why We Don't Believe (or, Don't Believe Our Own Testimony)

So the emergence of art as Art creates room to expand unbelief; unbelief has somewhere to go without settling for the mechanism of a completely flattened universe but also without returning to a traditional religion that is now implausible. This, obviously, is the Romantic option, one that remains alive and well in a "postmodern" context.

But the Enlightenment is still with us, too. Taylor diagnoses its endurance in a fragilized secular₃ age through a fascinating little psychoanalysis of a convert — but of someone (or a culture) that has converted from belief to unbelief. The upshot is a hermeneutics of suspicion; if someone tells you that he or she has converted to unbelief because of science, don't believe them. Because what's usually captured the person is not scientific evidence per se, but the *form* of science: "Even where the conclusions of science seem to be doing the work of conversion, it is very often not the detailed findings so much as the form" (p. 362). Indeed, "the appeal of scientific materialism is not so much the cogency of its detailed findings as that of the underlying epistemological stance, and that for ethical reasons. It is seen as the stance of maturity, of courage, of manliness, over against childish fears and sentimentality" (p. 365). But you can also understand how, on the retelling, the convert to unbelief will want to give the impression that it was the scientific evidence that was doing the work. Converts to unbelief always tell subtraction stories.

And the belief such persons have converted *from* has usually been an immature, Sunday-schoolish faith that could be easily toppled. So while such converts to unbelief tell themselves stories about "growing up" and "facing reality" — and thus paint belief as essentially immature and childish — their "testimony" betrays the simplistic shape of the faith they've abandoned. "If our faith has remained at the stage of the immature images, then the story that materialism equals maturity can seem plausible" (p. 365). But in fact, their conversion to unbelief was also a conversion to a new faith: "faith in science's ability" (p. 366).

Such tales of maturity and "growing up" to "face reality" are stories of courage — the courage to face the fact that the universe is without transcendent meaning, without eternal purpose, without supernatural significance. So the convert to unbelief has "grown up" because she can handle the truth that our disenchanted world is a cold, hard place. At the same time, there can be something exhilarating in this loss of purpose

Taylor suggests that those who convert to unbelief "because of science" are less convinced by data and more moved by the form of the *story* that science tells and the self-image that comes with it (rationality = maturity). Moreover, the faith that they left was often worth leaving. **If Taylor is right, it seems to suggest that the Christian response to such converts to unbelief is not to have an argument about the data or "evidences" but rather to offer an alternative story that offers a more robust, complex understanding of the Christian faith.** The goal of such witness would not be the minimal establishment of some vague theism but the invitation to historic, sacramental Christianity.

and teleology, because if nothing matters, and we have the courage to face this, then we have a kind of Epicurean invulnerability. While such a universe might have nothing to offer us by way of comfort, it's also true that "in such a universe, nothing is demanded of us" (p. 367). Now the loss of purpose is also a liberation: "*we* decide what goals to pursue." God is dead; *viva la revolution.*[22]

In the "liberating" power of the loss of meaning, one can already see burgeoning hints of what's coming: Nietzsche, and other "post-Schopenhauerian" visions (p. 369). What we get here, according to Taylor, is an internal critique of modernity, the "immanent counter-Enlightenment" that turns against the values of the Enlightenment precisely insofar as those values were secular analogues of a Christian inheritance (think: *Genealogy of Morals,* which targets Kant *and* Jesus, Hegel *and* Paul). What we get from Nietzsche is a critique of that strand of exclusive humanism that secularized agape, giving us the universalized "agape-analogue" (pp. 369-70; cp. 27). What we get from this Enlightenment formalization or secularization of Christian sensibilities is "a secular religion of life" (p. 371) — and it is *that* to which the post-Schopenhauerian strains of counter-Enlightenment are reacting.[23] On their account, Kant is still immature; still blind to the harsh realities of our cold, cruel universe; and thus still captive to slave morality, unable to be a hero (p. 373). This post-Schopenhauerian vision is still a minority report in contemporary Western culture, however. But one can see the countermovement already within modernity itself.

We have arrived at a new place in human history: "A race of humans has arisen which has managed to experience its world entirely as immanent. In some respect, we may judge this achievement as a victory for darkness, but it is a remarkable achievement nonetheless" (p. 376).

---

22. One gets the sense, however, that Taylor thinks there are diminishing returns on this: that something in the universe is going to keep pushing back, and that something in ourselves is not going to allow us to be satisfied with what looks like "freedom." One might suggest that Jonathan Franzen's *Freedom* gets at the same malaise.

23. I wonder whether one could read Michael Chabon's and Amy Chua's critiques of modern parenting as a kind of cultural expression of a similar reaction to the politics of politeness that we get from a secular religion of life.

CHAPTER 4

Contesting the Secularization$_2$ Thesis

In some ways, by the end of part 3, Taylor has brought us to the present. The history has largely been told; getting to the nineteenth century is pretty much all we need of a genealogy that will make sense of our present. (Taylor is often wont to talk about "our Victorian contemporaries.")[1] As we move into part 4, then, we move from history to analysis (though the distinction is always heuristic at best in Taylor's work).

Taylor's telling of the (his)story has already departed from the "standard story" about the path to our present — the standard story always being some version of a subtraction story. So in part 4 Taylor takes up themes and issues generally treated under the rubric of "secularization," giving an account of the decline of religious practice in the West. As he notes at the end of chapter 11, what he's particularly interested in is how religion has been decoupled from society and its institutions. However, he is going to take up these issues in a way that contests the usual "secularization$_2$ thesis," and to do so he revisits his earlier distinction between secularity$_1$, secularity$_2$, and secularity$_3$.[2]

1. Charles Taylor, *Sources of the Self* (Cambridge: Harvard University Press, 1989), pp. 393-417.

2. See the summary of this taxonomy in the introduction. I will generally refer to "the secularization$_2$ thesis" to flag that the "standard" secularization theory operates on the basis of the second notion of "the secular."

A Counternarrative: On Secularization$_2$ Theory

Just as secularity cannot be adequately explained by a *subtraction* story, neither can it be accounted for with a *diffusion* story — as if secularization was just the trickle-down effect of elite pluralism making its way to the masses (p. 424). Nor can it be adequately explained by just hitching it to some wagon of modern development such as differentiation, privatization, urbanization, industrialization, or disenchantment because of the simple fact that these phenomena did not empirically entail a decline in religious practice; indeed, they often occasioned their own kind of religious response and revival (pp. 425-26).

So to get at this issue, Taylor goes *meta;* that is, he steps back and starts asking more fundamental questions. For example, if secularization is taken to refer to some kind of "decline of religion," then we need to figure out what we mean by "religion." "If one identifies this with the great historic faiths, or even with explicit belief in supernatural beings, then it seems to have declined. But if you include a wide range of spiritual and semi-spiritual beliefs; or if you cast your net even wider and think of someone's religion as the shape of their ultimate concern, then indeed, one can make a case that religion is as present as ever" (p. 427).[3] Furthermore, what's the point of comparison? If secularization theory claims a decline in religious participation, "what is the past we are comparing ourselves with? Even in ages of faith, everybody wasn't really devout."

However, Taylor doesn't really follow up on these questions. Instead he goes *hermeneutical meta;* that is, he begins to interrogate the background assumptions operative behind secularization theory — what he calls (following Foucault) the **"unthought"** that "underpins much secularization theory" (p. 427). In this respect, Taylor challenges the myth of neutrality in the social sciences, but *not* with the supposedly "postmod-

---

3. I make the case for the latter in James K. A. Smith, "Secular Liturgies and the Prospects for a 'Post-Secular' Sociology of Religion," in *The Post-Secular in Question,* ed. Philip Gorski et al. (New York: NYU Press, 2012), pp. 159-84. One might also compare work on "implicit religion" in the UK. See, for example, Edward Bailey, *The Secular Faith Controversy: Religion in Three Dimensions* (London: Continuum, 2001), and Bailey, *Implicit Religion: An Introduction* (Bristol, UK: Centre for the Study of Implicit Religion, 1998). But Taylor later seems to affirm a rather traditional and narrow definition of "religion" (p. 429).

ern" conclusion that "we are each imprisoned in our own outlook, and can do nothing to rationally convince each other" (p. 428). His critique of neutrality and disclosure of presuppositions is not a license for retreating into our silos and choirs. Rather, Taylor remains confident that there can be dialogue and even persuasion *across* "unthoughts." Though he comes at secularity from a *different* unthought than those who espouse secularization$_2$ theory, "that doesn't mean that we have simply a stand-off here, where we make declarations to each other from out of our respective ultimate premises. Presumably, one or other view about religious aspiration can allow us to make better sense of what has actually happened. Being in one or other perspective makes it easier for some or other insights to come to you; but there is still the question of how these insights pan out in the actual account of history" (p. 436). For Taylor, the problem with secularization$_2$ theory is that it doesn't adequately account for the phenomena.

So Taylor is pointing out that any account of secularization is inevitably informed by some "unthought," some pretheoretical perspective that comes with a certain sensibility and orientation — what he calls "tempers" or "outlooks." Taylor crystallizes this with a kind of case study: one can see these different tempers manifest in what you think about Francis of Assisi, "with his renunciation of his potential life as a merchant, his austerities, his stigmata": "One can be deeply moved by this call to go beyond flourishing"; or "one can see him as a paradigm exemplar of what Hume calls 'the monkish virtues,' a practitioner of senseless self-denial and a threat to civil mutuality" (p. 431). Tell me what you think of Saint Francis, Taylor suggests, and I'll tell you what your "unthought" is.

What is the "unthought" of secularization$_2$ theorists — their background assumptions that shape their account of secularity? It is, Taylor suggests, "an outlook which holds that religion must decline either (a) because it is false, and science shows this to be so; or (b) because it is increasingly irrelevant now that we can cure ringworm by drenches [the 'artificial-fertilizers-make-atheists' argument]; or (c) because religion is based on authority, and modern societies give an increasingly important place to individual autonomy; or some combination of the above" (pp. 428-29). Some constellation of these assumptions is shared by academics even in countries like the United States where wider religious participation is very high — and it can't help but influence the story such academics tell about secularization. The result is an inevitably reductionistic account of religion that is unable to imagine that religion could be a true *motivator* for human action (pp. 433, 452-53).[4] It also tends to reduce religion to merely epiphenomenal beliefs about supernatural entities, and such beliefs disappear in the conditions of modernity (pp. 430, 433-34). If this is your "unthought," you'll tend to look at Saint Francis with rather pitiful eyes: that poor, benighted, misguided, but sincere soul (er, brain).

Taylor concedes that he has his own "unthought" (p. 429). "I stand in another perspective," he confesses. "I am moved by the life of Francis of Assisi, for instance; and that has something to do with why this [secularization$_2$ thesis] picture of the disappearance of independent religious inspiration seems to me so implausible" (p. 436). Indeed, "my own view of 'secularization,'" he freely admits, "has been shaped by my own perspective as a believer" (p. 437).

What difference does Taylor's (Catholic) "unthought" make? How does his temper or outlook provide a different perspective? Well, it entails two features: first, Taylor is willing to see religion as a genuine, independent, irreducible motivator for human action and social life — not something that can just be explained away as the epiphenomenon of economic or political or evolutionary factors (p. 453).[5] Second, Taylor does not reduce religion to mere belief in supernatural entities. Instead, he emphasizes that a **"transformation perspective"** is essential to religion — "the perspective of a transformation of human beings which takes them beyond or outside of whatever is normally understood as human flourishing" (p. 430). It is just this transformation perspective that impinges on the moral order; but it is also this transformation perspective that is cross-pressured in modernity. So religion isn't just about a set of propositional beliefs regarding certain kinds of supernatural entities; religion isn't merely an epistemology and a metaphysics. It is more fundamentally about a *way of life* — and a "religious" way of life, on Taylor's account, is

4. On this point, cp. Christian Smith's argument in *What Is a Person?* (Chicago: University of Chicago Press, 2010).

5. Compare Christian Smith's argument in *Moral, Believing Animals: Human Personhood and Culture* (Oxford: Oxford University Press, 2003).

one that calls us to more than the merely worldly, more than just "human flourishing."

What difference does this make in the account of secularization? Taylor *does* affirm that there has indeed been a process of secularization; he also recognizes that in much of the West, there has also been a decline in religious participation and identification. So contesting the secularization₂ thesis does not require rejecting those facts on the ground. Instead, it just means that Taylor offers a different story: "the heart of 'secularization'" is precisely "a decline in the transformation perspective" (p. 431). So while there has certainly been a decline of religion, that's not the most interesting story: "the interesting story is not simply one of decline, but also of a new placement of the sacred or spiritual in relation to individual and social life" (p. 437). It is this new *placement* of religion that is constitutive of our "secular age."[6] It's not just that belief in supernatural entities becomes implausible; it's that pursuing a way of life that values something beyond human flourishing becomes unimaginable.

Taylor locates his debate with the "mainstream secularization thesis" by likening it to a three-story building (pp. 431-33) (see figure 2):

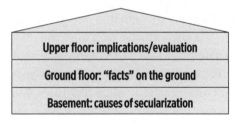

Figure 2. The "unthoughts" of secularization theory

Taylor often agrees with mainstream secularization theory "on the ground floor," so to speak. He can recognize the data about declining religious participation and so on. It's in the diagnosis of causes and evaluation that he disagrees. And this is because "it turns out that basement and higher

6. Elsewhere he describes this as a "recomposition" of religious life. See Taylor, "The Future of the Religious Past," in Taylor, *Dilemmas and Connections: Selected Essays* (Cambridge: Harvard University Press, Belknap Press, 2011), p. 228.

floor are intimately linked; that is, that the explanation one gives for the declines registered by 'secularization' relate closely to one's picture of the place of religion today" (p. 433). Indeed, it is precisely on the upper floor that the "unthought" exerts its force, and insofar as the upper floor drives us to posit corresponding causes, the "unthought" also exerts influence on our attribution of causality.

The Age of Authenticity

The Social Imaginary of Expressive Individualism

Taylor takes a stab at showing what difference his "take" might make by offering "an outrageously simplified potted history of the last two-and-some centuries" (p. 437). Classic Taylor (but we love him for it). The goal is to track the move from some elite unbelief in the eighteenth century to mass secularization in the twenty-first century. He does so by introducing what he calls "Weber-style ideal types" of religious forms at different stages. So, for example, we begin with the "**ancien régime**" (AR) type, where there is an inextricable link between religious identity and political identity — "a close connection between church membership and being part of a national, but particularly local community" (p. 440). The array of rituals that binds the polis or kingdom or nation together as a community also conscripts individual identities. But "religion of this kind is uniquely vulnerable to the defection of élites, since they are often in a position severely to restrict, if not put an end altogether to the central collective rituals" (p. 441). The disruptive effect of the Reformation in certain regions, for example, was due in no small part to the ability of the Reformers to convince princes.

Over time (and in much more complexity than we can summarize here), Taylor sees the AR leading to a new phase and type: the **Age of Mobilization** (AM). The status quo and ancien régime having been displaced, we now realize that if anything is going to fill the void, *we* need to come up with it — we will need to "mobilize" new rituals, practices, institutions, and so forth. The old "backdrop" is gone; "whatever political, social, ecclesial structures we aspire to have to be mobilized into existence"

(p. 445). There is no ancien régime we can take for granted, and no enchanted cosmos in which God resides and in which we are embedded. So religion (and religious identity) changes, too: God is now present in his design, in order. He will be similarly present in our polity, *if* we construct it aright, *if* we conform our constitution to the order God decrees in the heavens. "The divine isn't there in a King who straddles the planes. But it can be present to the extent that we build a society which plainly follows God's design. This can be filled in with an idea of moral order which is seen as established by God, in the way invoked, for instance, in the American Declaration of Independence" (p. 447) — the very embodiment of the "modern moral order" (MMO). Taylor suggests that the Age of Mobilization is roughly 1800-1960 (p. 471).[7]

Ours is the **Age of Authenticity** (AA).[8] So what we get in chapter 13 is Taylor's explication of "the social imaginary of expressive individualism" — the "understanding . . . that each one of us has his/her own way of realizing our humanity, and that it is important to find and live out one's own, as against surrendering to conformity with a model imposed on us from the outside" (p. 486). It is this unique form of the modern, post-Romantic social imaginary that has exploded "in the last half century, perhaps even less, which has profoundly altered the conditions of belief in our societies" (p. 473). What's at issue here is not so much the causes or mechanisms (Taylor will consistently point to the consumer revolution and postwar affluence; pp. 474, 490), but rather "the understandings of human life, agency, and the good" that emerge with this expansion of expressive individualism (p. 474). This contemporary social imaginary is crystallized in terms of *authenticity.* So the primary — yea, only — value in such a world is *choice:* "bare choice as a prime value, irrespective of what it is a choice between, or in what domain" (p. 478). And tolerance is the last remaining virtue: "the sin which is not tolerated is intolerance" (p. 484).

Taylor sees two temptations when it comes to our *evaluation* of the Age of Authenticity (p. 480): critics can too easily dismiss it as egoism; friends can too easily celebrate it as progress without cost. Taylor's evaluation

---

7. This would accord with the argument of Ross Douthat's *Bad Religion: How We Became a Nation of Heretics* (New York: Free Press, 2012). Taylor's "Age of Authenticity" — what follows AM — is synonymous with what Douthat might have called "the age of heresy."

8. This was also a core theme of Taylor's analysis in *Sources of the Self.*

takes a different tack: on his reading, the AA has changed our available options — it has changed not just the conditions of belief but the milieu of our everyday lived experience.

To get at this, he homes in on fashion as a bit of a case study. While fashion is a medium of *expression* for my individuality, it is also inescapably relational, almost parasitic: "The space of fashion is one in which we sustain a language together of signs and meanings, which is constantly changing, but which at any moment is the background needed to give our gestures the sense they have" (p. 481). This is no longer a space of common action but rather a space of *mutual display* — another way of "being-with" in which "a host of urban monads hover on the boundary between solipsism and communication" (p. 482). This breeds a new kind of self-consciousness: "My loud remarks and gestures are overtly addressed only to my immediate companions, my family group is sedately walking, engaged in our own Sunday outing, but all the time we are aware of this common space that we are building, in which the messages that cross take their meaning" (p. 482). In other words, we all behave now like thirteen-year-old girls.[9]

It is these spaces of mutual display, Taylor argues, that are most prone to being colonized by consumer culture, so that "consumer culture, expressivism and spaces of mutual display connect in our world to produce their own kind of synergy" (p. 483): "The language of self-definition is defined in the spaces of mutual display, which have now gone meta-topical; they relate us to prestigious centres of style-creation, usually in rich and powerful nations and milieux. And this language is the object of constant attempted manipulation by large corporations" (p. 483). Indeed, this construction of a consumer identity — which has to *feel* like it's chosen (consider the illusion of nonconformity in the case of the suburban skater kid whose mom buys him the $150 board blazoned with "anarchy" symbols) — *trumps* other identities, especially collective identities like citizenship or religious affiliation.[10] "One could argue that for many young people to-

---

9. In *Imagining the Kingdom: How Worship Works* (Grand Rapids: Baker Academic, 2013), pp. 146-48, I have compared this with David Foster Wallace's account of our self-conscious age of expressive individualism.

10. Cp. Kenda Creasy Dean, *Almost Christian: What the Faith of Our Teenagers Is Telling the American Church* (New York: Oxford University Press, 2010).

day, certain styles, which they enjoy and display in their more immediate circle, but which are defined through the media, in relation to admired stars — or even products — occupy a bigger place in their sense of self, and that this has tended to displace in importance the sense of belonging to large scale collective agencies, like nations, not to speak of churches, political parties, agencies of advocacy, and the like" (p. 484).

This expansion of expressive individualism does not unsettle the modern moral order; if anything, it strengthens the order of mutual benefit. Indeed, the MMO is the "ethical base" for the soft relativism of the expressivist imaginary: Do your own thing, who am I to judge? The only sin is intolerance. *Here* is where Taylor locates the most significant shift in the post-'60s West: while ideals of tolerance have always been present in the modern social imaginary, in earlier forms (Locke, the early American republic, etc.) this value was contained and surrounded by other values that were a scaffolding of formation (e.g., the citizen ethic; p. 484). What erodes in the last half century is precisely these limits on individual fulfillment (p. 485).

The Place of the Sacred in Our Secular Age

What is the "imagined place of the sacred" in a society governed by expressivist individualism (p. 486)? Taylor has already hinted that such a society seems to forge its own "festive" rendition of the sacred — "moments of fusion in a common action/feeling, which both wrench us out of the everyday, and seem to put us in touch with something exceptional, beyond ourselves. Which is why some have seen these moments as among the new forms of religion in our world" (pp. 482-83).[11] But while there might still be room for a kind of sacred, something has also clearly changed. Taylor's taxonomy can be mapped onto the earlier types of religious identity (AR, AM, AA):

- Under the dispensation of the AR, "my connection to the sacred entailed my belonging to the church," and the church (Roman Catholic,

---

11. Cp. Dreyfus and Kelly on the role of sport (and the "whoosh"), in *All Things Shining: Reading the Western Classics to Find Meaning in a Secular Age* (New York: Free Press, 2011).

87

Lutheran, Anglican) is coextensive with society such that there is "a link between adhering to God and belonging to the state" (p. 486).

- In the AM, there has been some disembedding. Here we see the emergence of the "denominational imaginary" (p. 450) and an emphasis on voluntary association, but when you join "the church of your choice," you're still connecting to something bigger — "the church" and its heritage, which still feeds and fuels the project of the nation.

- But now in the AA, with its expressive individualist outlook, we have a qualitative shift: "The religious life or practice that I become part of must not only be my choice, but it must speak to me, it must make sense in terms of my spiritual development as I understand this" (p. 486). The expressivist forges her own religion ("spirituality"), her own, personal Jesus.[12] But what's most significant is that the sacred is uncoupled from political allegiance (p. 487). This begins to loosen up things more generally, in accord with expressivist individualism, such that it becomes less and less "rational" to accept any external constraints. So whereas Methodists and Pietists unleash an emphasis on emotional encounters with God but keep this tethered to orthodoxy, it is only a matter of time "before the emphasis will shift more and more towards the strength and the genuineness of the feelings, rather than the nature of their object" (p. 488). And so a new spiritual injunction arises: "let everyone follow his/her own path of spiritual inspiration. Don't be led off yours by the allegation that it doesn't fit with some orthodoxy" (p. 489).

Taylor's account of the secular is often an illuminating lens through which to see changes *within* religious communities, not just the expansion of the areligious. **How might his account here provide a lens through which to understand the so-called emerging church and other forms of anti-institutionalism in contemporary Christianity?**

12. I would like to suggest that Johnny Cash's cover of this Depeche Mode song does a masterful job of ironically calling into question the very notion of your own "personal Jesus" — as if to say, why the *hell* would I want a Jesus cut to my preference? Which is why *American IV* includes "The Man Comes Around" and *American V* includes "God's Gonna Cut You Down." Would my own personal Jesus do *that*?

What draws people away from traditional, institutional religion is largely the success of consumer culture — the "stronger form of magic" found in the ever-new glow of consumer products (p. 490). As a result, the expressivist revolution (1) "undermined some of the large-scale religious forms of the Age of Mobilization" and (2) "undermined the link between Christian faith and civilizational order" (p. 492). In fact, "where the link between disciplines and civilizational order is broken, but that between Christian faith and the disciplines remains unchallenged, expressivism and the conjoined sexual revolution has alienated many people from the churches" (p. 493).

The Quest: Spirituality in the Age of Authenticity

What does *religion* look like in the Age of Authenticity (AA)? "What is the spiritual life like which emerges from the expressive revolution?" (p. 506).

It is first worth noting that a desire for "the spiritual" endures. "This often springs from a profound dissatisfaction with a life encased entirely in the immanent order" (p. 506). So the spiritual migrates, as it were. As a result, AA spirituality is a *quest* for the individual. Nothing is given or axiomatic anymore, so one has to "find" one's faith: "I have to discover my route to wholeness and spiritual depth. The focus is on the individual, and on his/her experience" (p. 507). This can explain phenomena like the widespread fascination with *The Lord of the Rings* (in film form, at least) or best-selling works like Paulo Coelho's novel *The Alchemist* or Elizabeth Gilbert's *Eat, Pray, Love.*[13]

What should we make of this form of spirituality? Taylor cautions, what one thinks of this depends on one's fundamental attitude about the nature of spirituality. In other words, our evaluation of this AA mode of spiritual expression will once again be informed by our different "un-thoughts." So in seeking to answer this question, Taylor regularly rebuffs the ham-fisted criticisms of traditionalists who simply lament the subjectivism and individualism of AA spirituality (e.g., pp. 508-9). This devolves

---

13. For a masterful reading of Gilbert and just the sort of expressivist spirituality Taylor is describing, see Douthat, *Bad Religion*, pp. 211-30.

into all sorts of false dichotomies either from militant secularists or from staunch religionists: "Each is comforted in their position by the thought that the only alternative is so utterly repulsive." But as usual, Taylor thinks things are messier than this and that such dichotomies "miss a good part of the spiritual reality of our age" (p. 509).

For example, it might be that traditional religions call into question the individualism and subjectivism of AA questing, pushing a more communal, teleological account of human flourishing. From their perspective, the "spirituality" of the AA seeker looks indulgent and self-centered — the typical egoistic preference for "spirituality" over "religion" that keeps the self ensconced as the center of the universe. However, Taylor cautions that we need to distinguish between the *framework* of AA spirituality and the *content* of such spirituality. As he puts it, "the new framework has a strongly individualist component, but this will not necessarily mean that the content will be individuating" (p. 516). In other words, while the spiritual seeker in our secular age is on an individual quest, that quest might actually end up with a conversion to Roman Catholicism that cuts against the libertarian individualism of the quest itself (p. 509). The Taizé Community and World Youth Day are cases in point: the "spiritual" quest ends in "religion" for these young people (pp. 509, 517).

But what we can't seem to escape, Taylor points out, is the quest-like shape of our searches in the present age. So while some "conservative souls" might lament this point, it might simply be inescapable (pp. 512-13). This is the correlate to Taylor's claim that there's no turning back the clock on disenchantment. Similarly, ours *is* an age of authenticity; it is our milieu, and even if we emerge into identities that call into question the expressivism and individualism of "authenticity," we can't escape the fact that we live in an age that makes this an *option.* And so we get the ironic reality: we choose to renounce the priority of individual choice; our quest leads us back to the ancien régime. That is what it means to live in a secular$_3$ age.

Furthermore, Taylor is not sure we should *want* to turn back the clock. "If ours tends to multiply somewhat shallow and undemanding spiritual options, we shouldn't forget the spiritual costs of various kinds of forced conformity: hypocrisy, spiritual stultification, inner revolt against the Gospel, the confusion of faith and power, and even worse. Even if we had a choice," Taylor muses, "I'm not sure we wouldn't be wiser to stick with the present dispensation" (p. 513).

The upshot is that in a secular$_3$ age, "committed secularism remains the creed of a relatively small minority" (p. 520). Because our past is irrevocably Christian (here's another Hegelian point), our secular$_3$ age continues to be "haunted" by this past, for example, at moments of rites of passage or in times of disaster, etc. (pp. 520-21): "people may retain an attachment to a perspective of transformation which they are not presently acting on . . . like a city FM station in the countryside" whose reception fades in and out (p. 521). To the extent that we are willing to recognize this, and refuse the "standard" story of secularization$_2$, we will find ourselves in a "postsecular" age, "a time in which the hegemony of the mainstream master narrative of secularization will be more and more challenged" (p. 534).[14] And, he continues, "this I think is now happening" (p. 535).

14. For further discussion of the "postsecular," see *The Post-Secular in Question.*

CHAPTER 5

How (Not) to Live in a Secular Age

The Immanent Frame

Having offered an alternative history in parts 1-3, and contesting the standard accounts of "how we got here" in part 4, in part 5 (the focus of this chapter) Taylor moves from history and genealogy to critical analysis. We might describe this as the "constructive" part of his project, but it's also where Taylor goes on offense, taking on the smug confidence of "secularist spin" — *not* in an apologetic mode of thereby smugly and confidently "proving" Christianity to be true, but instead undercutting the confidence of the secularist "take" on the world, showing it to *be* a take, a construal, a reading. In sum, the final part of *A Secular Age* is an attempt to get secularists$_2$ to own up to inhabiting a secular$_3$ age.

It is in this context that Taylor coins what will be a crucial concept going forward: the **immanent frame**. This metaphorical concept — alluding to a "frame" that both boxes in *and* boxes out, encloses *and* focuses — is meant to capture the world we now inhabit in our secular age: "this frame constitutes a 'natural' order, to be contrasted to a 'supernatural' one, an 'immanent' world, over against a possible 'transcendent' one" (p. 542).[1]

---

1. Taylor goes on to argue that the very natural/supernatural distinction is itself an effect of the immanent frame (pp. 542, 548). So those believers who strenuously seek to defend the "supernatural" and the "intervention" of transcendence are already conceding the paradigm of the immanent frame (which is why this is "a view of things shared between

We now inhabit this self-sufficient immanent order, *even if we believe in transcendence.* Indeed, Taylor emphasizes the ubiquity of the immanent frame: it is "common to all of us in the modern West" (p. 543). So the question isn't *whether* we inhabit the immanent frame, but *how.* Some inhabit it as a closed frame with a brass ceiling; others inhabit it as an open frame with skylights open to transcendence.

At this point, Taylor is interested in two dynamics:

1. What "tips" our orientation within the immanent frame? Why are some inclined to *live* as if it were closed? What inclines others to inhabit it as if it were open? What *motivates* these different stances (p. 548)? Whence these two different "basic orientations"? Note the existential emphasis here: this is not treated as a question of knowledge or belief, but rather as a question of how we *live* in the immanent frame, the forms of life we pursue within it. It is the lived question of *how,* not the spectator's question of *what.*

2. And then a more *meta*-question: Why do some not recognize that their construal of the frame as open or closed is just that — a *construal,* a "take" on things? In particular, why do secularists so confidently assume that this is just "the way things are" — the "obvious" and only thing to conclude?

Let's begin with the second concern, which is Taylor's focus in the early parts of chapter 15, and which also provides clues to answering the first question.

"Takes" on Transcendence and "Spins" in the Frame

Taylor argues that *how* one inhabits the immanent frame hinges on just how one construes transcendence: Do you see the transcendent as "a

materialists and Christian Fundamentalists," p. 547), whereas an earlier understanding would have resisted the distinction — not in the direction of a naturalism but precisely in a more complex picture of an enchanted world, a "charged" cosmos. Not surprisingly, Taylor often expresses sympathy with Henri de Lubac on this score.

threat, a dangerous temptation, a distraction, or an obstacle to our greatest good"? Or do you see the transcendent as "answering to our deepest craving, need, fulfillment of the good" (p. 548)?

However, the problem is that this question is not usually put to us in just this way, and we don't often articulate a "position" on these matters. This is because, "not only is the immanent frame itself not usually, or even mainly a set of *beliefs* which we entertain about our predicament, however it may have started out; rather [the immanent frame] is the sensed context in which we develop our beliefs." We don't have a "position" on transcendence; instead, we have a "take" on things within the immanent frame, and such a "take" "has usually sunk to the level of such an unchallenged framework, something we have trouble often thinking ourselves outside of, even as an imaginative exercise" (p. 549). In other words, this take seeps into our social imaginary; it becomes part of the background that governs our being-in-the-world.

Thus Taylor suggests that our basic motivations or orientations within the immanent frame are not necessarily ratiocinative conclusions that we've thought through. *How* you inhabit the immanent frame is less a fruit of deduction and more a "vibe." It is less a reasoned position or articulated worldview and more a Wittgensteinian "picture"[2] that holds us captive precisely because it's not conscious. It is a "background to our thinking, within whose terms it is carried on, but which is often largely unformulated, and to which we can frequently, just for this reason, imagine no alternative" (p. 549).

So again, the question is *how* we inhabit the immanent frame. And here Taylor works with another important distinction: we can either inhabit the immanent frame as a "Jamesian open space"[3] where we recognize the contestability of our *take* on things, and even feel the pull and tug and cross-pressure of the alternative; *or* we'll fail to recognize that ours is

2. For a related discussion, see Charles Taylor, "Merleau-Ponty and the Epistemological Picture," in *The Cambridge Companion to Merleau-Ponty*, ed. Taylor Carman and Mark B. N. Hansen (Cambridge: Cambridge University Press, 2005), pp. 26-49.

3. Taylor is referring to William James's description of an existentially "open space where you can feel the winds pulling you, now to belief, now to unbelief" (p. 549). Taylor explores this further in his lectures on James published as *The Varieties of Religion Today* (Cambridge: Harvard University Press, 2003).

a "take" and instead settle for "**spin**" — an overconfident "picture" within which we can't imagine it being otherwise, and thus smugly dismiss those who disagree. If we settle for "spin," we'll think it's just "obvious" that the frame is open or closed. Thus "what I am calling 'spin,'" Taylor summarizes, "is a way of avoiding entering this [Jamesian] space, a way of convincing oneself that one's reading is obvious, compelling, allowing of no cavil or demurral" (p. 551).[4]

We might imagine a matrix of options here:

	TAKE	SPIN
(Transcendence) Open	Charles Taylor	(religious fundamentalisms)
(Immanence) Closed	(Julian Barnes?)	"the Academy"

Figure 3. "Takes" and "spin": A matrix of options

Taylor is most interested in considering (and contesting) the "spin of closure which is hegemonic in the Academy" (p. 549). This is the spin that is dominant amongst intellectuals and elites who would actually see the "open" take on the immanent frame *as* "spin" and see their own "closed" take as *just the way things are.* For these secular "fundamentalists," we might say, to construe the immanent frame as closed is to just see it as it *really* is, whereas construing it as "open" is a mode of wishful thinking. In effect they say: we "closed" framers are just facing up to the facts of the case; it's "open" framers who are *interpreting* the world *as if* it could be open. The immanent frame is *really* closed even if some persist in *construing* it as open (p. 550). For those adherents of the closed reading, *it's not a "reading."*

In contrast, Taylor argues that the immanent frame is underdetermined, susceptible to two different takes or construals: "it allows both readings, without compelling us to either." Indeed, "if you grasp our pre-

---

4. To have this stance is to be hamstrung in a way: "those who think the closed reading of immanence is 'natural' and obvious are suffering from this kind of disability" (p. 551), though there could be transcendent "spin" as well.

dicament without ideological distortion, and without blinders, then you see that going one way or another requires what is often called a 'leap of faith' " (p. 550).

The closed blindness to this reality partly stems from the intellectual subtraction stories they tell themselves — that they hold to the "closed" view as a rational conclusion and an Enlightened "position." But again Taylor's more affective epistemology (or better, hermeneutics) points out that our "take" is not something reasoned *to* as much as it is something we reason *from*. It is an "over-all sense of things" that "anticipates or leaps ahead of the reasons we can muster for it. It is something in the nature of a hunch" or what we might call "anticipatory confidence" (p. 550). While there can be increases in confidence, "we never move to a point beyond all anticipation, beyond all hunches, to the kind of certainty we can enjoy in certain narrower questions, say, in natural science or ordinary life" (p. 551).[5]

A lot of contemporary apologetics, bent on "defending the faith" against the charges of the new atheists, seem to offer a transcendent "spin" as the alternative to immanent "spin." **What might a Christian apologetic look like that offers a transcendent "take" on our experience, even at points recognizing the force and persuasive power of an immanent "take"?**

So secularist spin is in fact the denial of contestability and thus the refusal to recognize secularity$_3$. Secularist spin fails to honor and recognize the cross-pressure that inhabitants of our secular age sense. The frame is not essentially or inherently "tipped" one way or the other. "The actual experience of living within Western modernity tends to awaken protest, resistances of various kinds. In this fuller, experiential sense, 'living within' the frame doesn't simply tip you in one direction, but allows you to feel pulled two ways. A very common experience of living here is that of being cross-pressured between the open and closed perspectives" (p. 555).

We could get a sense of this by returning to Taylor's case of Saint

---

5. This last qualifier seems a bit odd — in addition to seemingly insulating natural science from this hermeneutic anticipation, who on earth thinks we operate with certainty in "ordinary life"?

Francis. Just as one's perspective on Saint Francis discloses one's "un-thought," so one's reaction to Saint Francis could test whether one has a closed "take" or a decidedly closed, immanentist "spin." Or let's take a more recent example: the case of Dolores Hart, whose story is narrated in the HBO documentary *God Is the Bigger Elvis*. Hart was a rising starlet in the '50s and early '60s, appearing in roles alongside Elvis and others such as Marlon Brando and Warren Beatty. She was enjoying the dream life that the myth of "Hollywood" promised. And then in 1963 she abandoned all that, and even a promise of marriage, to become a Benedictine nun. She has lived at the Abbey of Regina Laudis in Bethlehem, Connecticut, ever since, and now serves as mother prioress. One can imagine what sort of account of this would be generated by closed spin — just consider Christopher Hitchens's excoriating book on Mother Teresa.[6] But interestingly, that's not what we get in the HBO documentary. Indeed, the documentary is a refreshing example of a closed take. The point of view is respectfully puzzled, admiringly incredulous. On the one hand, Hart's journey and choice seem unimaginable, almost unintelligible; on the other hand, they testify to a "something more" that holds the attention of both the director and the viewers. The film inhabits the "Jamesian open space" that Taylor describes, and inhabits it in a way that refuses spin.

Closed World Structures (CWSs)

Taylor returns to a promised analysis (p. 551) of "*closed* world structures" (CWSs) — those aspects of our contemporary experience that "tip" the immanent frame toward a *closed* construal.[7] In doing so, Taylor is actually bent on demythologizing the supposed "naturalness" of this take (spin?), showing us "the illusion of the rational 'obviousness' of the closed per-spective" (p. 556). Such supposed obviousness is an attempt to insulate us from the "fragilization" of our secular age.[8]

---

6. Christopher Hitchens, *The Missionary Position: Mother Teresa in Theory and Practice*, unabridged ed. (New York: The Twelve, 2012).

7. "World" in the Heideggerian sense of a constituted environment (p. 556). The CWSs are almost akin to Heideggerian *existentiale*.

8. Taylor packs a lot into an important note on fragilization: fragilization is the effect

Epistemology as a Functional CWS

Taylor is interested in how such CWSs *function:* what they do to us and how they shape our experience — how they "tip" the immanent frame, loading the deck as it were, and thus constraining our construal. But before considering four CWSs, he takes a bit of a detour through a (related) case: the shape of modern epistemology (philosophy of knowledge).[9] The shift to a modern, foundationalist epistemology, Taylor suggests, operates *as* a CWS because of how it structures knowledge; beginning with the certainty of my representations, there is a kind of concentric circle of certitude. "This can operate as a CWS because it is obvious that the inference to the transcendent is at the extreme and most fragile end of a chain of inferences; it is the most epistemically questionable" (p. 558). If knowledge is knowing something "outside" my mind, the transcendent would seem to be as far away as one could get. This loads the dice against any expectation of making contact, and the whole notion becomes more and more implausible.

But if modern epistemology is a kind of parallel CWS, then the *critique* of such an epistemology in Heidegger and Merleau-Ponty provides a clue to what a critique

---

If the foundationalist paradigm in epistemology is itself a "closed world structure," tipping us in the direction of a closed take, then isn't it ironic that so many Christian apologists are committed to a foundationalist conception of reason and hence a "classical" apologetics? Such Christian responses already cede ground to a "closed" take. **What would an "open" epistemology look like, and what sort of apologetic would it engender? Might nonfoundationalism in epistemology already testify to an "opening" in the immanent frame? In that case, might postmodernism be an ally of Christianity rather than a threat?**

---

of "the greater proximity of alternatives" that "has led to a society in which more people change their positions, that is, 'convert' in their lifetimes, and/or adopt a different position than their parents" (p. 833 n. 19). But contra Berger, "this has nothing to do with a supposed greater fragility of the faith they end up with (or decide to remain with), as Berger seems to imply. On the contrary, the faith arising in this contemporary predicament can be stronger, just because it has faced the alternative without distortion" (p. 834).

9. This parallels his essay "Overcoming Epistemology," in *Philosophical Arguments* (Cambridge: Harvard University Press, 1995).

of CWSs in general would look like (pp. 558-60). In other words, hermeneutic phenomenology's critique of foundationalism and correspondence theories of truth should also underwrite a critique of closed spin. In particular, this critique calls into question the neutrality and "naturalness" of this take on knowledge — and in doing so calls into question a *lot* of the status quo in the contemporary industry of analytic philosophy that often underwrites the rabid naturalism that dominates contemporary philosophy.[10] "From within itself, the epistemological picture seems unproblematic. It comes across as an obvious discovery we make when we reflect on our perception and acquisition of knowledge." Descartes, Locke, and Hume have finally "seen" what was there all along. But "seen from the deconstruction [of Heidegger et al.], this [obviousness] is [actually] a most massive self-blindness. Rather what happened is that experience was carved into shape by a powerful *theory* which posited the primacy of the individual, the neutral, the intra-mental as the locus of certainty" (p. 559, emphasis added). In fact, Taylor points out, undergirding this epistemological theory is actually a *moral* valuation: "There is an ethic here, of independence, self-control, self-responsibility, of a disengagement which brings control" (p. 559). So the theory is value-laden and parades itself as "a stance which requires courage, the refusal of the easy comforts of conformity to authority, of the consolations of an enchanted world, of the surrender to the promptings of the senses" (p. 560).

Here we see two key aspects of Taylor's critique of CWSs. (1) What pretends to be a "discovery" of the way things are, the "obvious" unveiling of reality once we remove (subtract) myth and enchantment, is *in fact* a construction, a *creation;* in short, this wasn't just a subtraction project. (2) Baseline *moral* commitments stand behind CWSs, specifically the coming-of-age metaphor of *adulthood,* having the courage to resist the comforting enchantments of childhood. In short, to just "see" the closedness of the immanent frame is to be a grown-up. Secular spin, in this way, is associated with maturity: "modernity as adulthood" (p. 588). But that is a *story,* not neutral data, and Taylor has been contesting such self-congratulatory stories all along.

---

10. How ironic, then, for Christian philosophers to challenge naturalism by employing the epistemological framework that is so closely linked to it.

"The Death of God" as a Constellation of CWSs

Taylor takes "the death of God" as a way to encapsulate a "constellation" of CWSs — a kind of "package deal" that tips us toward a closed, immanentist take on our experience. The phrase simply captures the sense that "conditions have arisen in the modern world in which it is no longer possible, honestly, rationally, without confusions, or fudging, or mental reservation, to believe in God" (p. 560). So "the death of God" is not necessarily only Nietzschean zealotry; rather, Taylor's point is that "the death of God" is more like a practical reality for many in our secular age who have never read Nietzsche. The death of God is seen as an effect of the deliverances of science and the shape of contemporary moral experience.

First, science tips toward materialism and is accompanied by a "just-so" story that issues in regretful, nostalgic, but brave "conversions" to exclusive humanism (pp. 563-64). As we've already noted, what's at stake in this invocation of "science" is less an account of empirical data and more an "ethic," a stance taken with respect to the world. "The convert to the new ethics has learned to mistrust some of his own deepest instincts, and in particular those which draw him to religious belief. . . . The crucial change is in the status accorded to the inclination to believe; this is the object of a radical shift in interpretation. It is no longer the impetus in us towards truth, but has become rather the most dangerous temptation to sin against the austere principles of belief-formation" (p. 563).

What Taylor questions is the supposed "discovery" here: "what is being claimed is that some move is being passed off as a simple discovery, which in fact is much more like a new construction." The "proponents of the death of God want to see Godlessness as a property of the universe which science lays bare," but in fact this too is a *take,* a construal, a *making* of a "world" (p. 565).

And for Taylor, the "arguments" don't really hold up. So why are people captivated by this story? What makes them convert? How do we account for the power of bad arguments (p. 567)? Well, first, Taylor thinks that really such conversions are conversions to a *new* authority, not the assumption of intellectual independence. There is a force to the *ethical* story behind the scientific just-so story: *Who doesn't want to be a grown-up?* But here Taylor also introduces the Desdemona analogy.[11] The point is that other sources/accounts are silenced; we hear only Iago's account, so "Desdemona's voice must be very faint within the modern horizon," suffering "from the blight of systemic mistrust" (p. 568).[12]

Second, exclusive humanism sets up a dichotomy between religion (Christianity) and humanism. "You can't be fully into contemporary humanist concerns if you haven't sloughed off the old beliefs. You can't be fully with the modern age and still believe in God" (p. 572). So anyone who wants to be "with it" — who wants to share her friends' humanist concerns about justice — is going to feel pressured to abandon faith and adopt a "closed" take. But Taylor calls into question this false dichotomy; it's not Christianity versus exclusive humanism, but rather Christian humanism versus exclusive humanism.[13]

As Taylor's been emphasizing, there's a *moral* to this just-so story of scientific materialism. It assumes an account of the emergence of modernity itself — what Taylor calls "the view from Dover Beach" (alluding to Arnold). This is primarily a subtraction story whereby "the transition to modernity comes about through the loss of traditional beliefs and allegiances" (p. 570). We *discover* that we are alone in the universe, and if there's going to be any meaning, *we* have to *make* it. But again, this story of unveiling and discovery and "facing up to reality" masks the fundamental *invention* of modernity. "What this view reads out of the picture is the possibility that Western modernity might be powered by its own positive visions of the good, that is, by one constellation of such visions

---

11. From Shakespeare's *Othello:* Desdemona is killed by her estranged husband, Othello, because he only listens to the information provided by Iago, who convinces Othello that Desdemona is an adulteress. (Recall Iago in Disney's *Aladdin*!)

12. But Taylor also notes the opposite possibility in this context: "Something like the vision which Dostoyevsky had in the Musuem in Basel before the *Dead Christ* by Hans Holbein, of the absolute finality of death, which convinced him that there must be something more, might easily have the opposite effect, of dragging you down and forcing an abandonment of your faith" (p. 569). The Prince in Dostoyevsky's novel *The Idiot* says of the painting: "Some people may lose their faith by looking at that picture" (cited p. 836 n. 33).

13. And exclusive humanism has a hard time accounting for the demands of universal justice and benevolence relying only on immanent sources ("the problem of good") (p. 572). Cp. Nicholas Wolterstorff's critique of "secular" (i.e., exclusive humanist) accounts of rights/justice in *Justice: Rights and Wrongs* (Princeton: Princeton University Press, 2008).

among available others, rather than by the only viable set left after the old myths and legends have been exploded." This is why Taylor seems to suggest that it is the *moral* force of the "scientific" story that lends it its authority, not the "evidence" (which most don't evaluate but rather take on testimony/authority). The "discovery" story line "naturalizes" the features of "modern, liberal identity. They cannot see it as one, historically constructed understanding of human agency among others" (p. 571). In short, they don't recognize it as a "take."[14]

But in a way, the "master narrative" of exclusive humanism has no room to be merely a take. Instead, it is "a story of great moral enthusiasm at a discovery, at a liberation from a narrower world of closer, claustrophobic relations, involving excessive control and invidious distinctions" (p. 575) — in other words, sophomore year writ large! — ignorant of the fact that others experience this "liberation" as "a catastrophic breakdown of the most crucial and elementary social bond" (p. 576).[15] The power of *attraction* to this story is "the positive attraction of the space we are released into" (p. 577). The goal, he says, is to be "Xer than thou" (p. 578).[16]

In this newly fashioned world, closed to anything transcendent, we are left alone without meaning; if there's to be meaning, it's something we have to *make.* Such a situation can be exhilarating: "we can be struck by the sense that we stand, as it were, before a normative abyss [*Garden State!*], that this blind, deaf, silent universe offers *no* guidance whatever; we can find here an exhilarating challenge, which inspires us, which can

14. An important methodological excursus here: While Taylor is trying to remythologize the demythologizers and enchant the disenchanters by pointing out the contingency and construal-based nature of their accounts, this is *not* meant to undercut the force of their construals per se. He just wants to pull the rug out from under their claims to "obviousness" — to unveil their "spin" and press them to recognize that the best they can offer is a "take." Indeed, he emphasizes: "if I can manage to tell this story properly, then we will see that there is some, phenomenal, truth to the 'death of God' account" (p. 836 n. 41).

15. Indeed, Taylor seems to be suggesting that this "liberation" just might not be conducive to human flourishing. Do we really need to look very far for confirmation of that intuition? For a literary depiction of this worry, read just about anything by Tom Wolfe. But see also Christopher Lasch's persistent critique of "liberationist" paradigms of liberalism.

16. Again, it seems to me that, perhaps unwittingly, this is *precisely* the myth called into question in Franzen's *Freedom* (including the "Xer than thou" dynamic that besets Patty).

even awaken a sense of the strange beauty of this alien universe, in the fact of which we stake our claim as legislators of meaning" (p. 581). But it can also be terrifying, and it's tough to shake our habits of acceding to external authorities to determine the good.

Once again there is a moral construal of relevant virtues at work here: in the face of this anonymity and silence of the universe, "some kind of decision is called for. And this decision requires a certain kind of courage; because so deeply ingrained in our history and culture, perhaps even in our make-up, is the connection between higher source and overriding claim, that the debunking of all outside sources can easily induce in us a failure of nerve" (p. 581). Kudos to us; we did it our way.

But if we are left to our own self-authorization, there is still a choice to make. In the face of this decision, we can choose either a remade humanism — as Camus and Derrida did (pp. 582-86) — *or* a more radical self-authorization, a Nietzschean revaluation of value that has even more courage: to jettison humanism as well (pp. 586-87). "So we see that the narrative of self-authorization can be told in many registers, some very radical. But the story is often told without distinguishing between these different forms, as a kind of generic story, pointing to the obvious fact, with the demise of God and the meaningful cosmos, we are the only authorizing agency left" (pp. 587-88). But "the narratives of self-authorization, when examined more closely, are far from self-evident; and yet their assuming axiomatic status in the thinking of many people, is one facet of a powerful and widespread CWS, imposing a closed spin on the immanent frame we all share" (p. 589). This isn't a theory that we're convinced of; it is a basic orientation that seeps into our bones, into our social imaginary.

Cross-Pressures: Faith in a Secular Age

Note that Taylor sees the cross-pressure not issuing so much from immanence and transcendence per se, but rather as a pressure "between the draw of narratives of closed immanence on one side, and the sense of their inadequacy on the other" (p. 595). "We are torn between an anti-Christian thrust and a repulsion towards some (to us) extreme form of reduction" (p. 599). So the cross-pressure issues from a vaguer sense of resistance, even "revulsion" and "recoil" with respect to the reduction-ism of closure ("Is that all there is?"). There is a fundamental discomfort with materialism and its attendant reductionism that generates a resis-tance and unwillingness to settle for the closed accounts of materialism (p. 595). Indeed, he suggests that this sort of cross-pressure "defines the whole culture," which is not to say that most people aren't "ensconced in a relatively untroubled way in one or other position" (p. 598).

Here Taylor returns to an important term for him: "fullness." This is a functional metaphor to name a "something more" that cross-pressures us. So "the uneasy sense" expressed by various resistances to reduction-ism and closure "is that the reductive materialist account of human be-ings leaves no place for fullness as they understand it" (p. 596). Taylor leaves this fullness underdetermined, to be sure, since he's looking for a kind of "ecumenical" term that need not be inherently religious or even necessarily transcendent (since "many of those who share this negative reaction to materialism also want to define themselves against ortho-dox religion, or at least Christianity" [pp. 596-97]). So "fullness" is not code for "God"; nonetheless, Taylor takes it "as axiomatic that everyone, and hence all philosophical positions, accept some definition of great-ness and fullness in human life" (p. 597). It is this fullness — or at least the felt need for fullness — that won't let us off the hook and leaves us cross-pressured.

Taylor identifies three "fields" of cross-pressure to which he will keep returning in chapter 16 (p. 596):

1. *Agency:* "the sense that we aren't just determined, that we are active, building, creating, shaping agents";

2. *Ethics:* "we have higher spiritual/ethical motives" that don't reduce to biological instinct or "base" drives; and

3. *Aesthetics:* "Art, Nature moves us" because of a sense of meaning; these are not just differential responses to pleasure.

Because Taylor thinks "there is no escaping *some* version of . . . fullness," our debates are really about "what real fullness consists in" (p. 600). He suggests that what's really at issue here is the telos of human life, "the ends of life" (p. 602). In other words, the debate about "real fullness" is a debate about how to understand our "ethical predicament": What counts as "fulfillment" (playing on "fullness")?

It is here that Taylor's argument seems to take a decidedly "apologetic" turn, pressing the question of whether "closed" takes on the immanent frame have sufficient resources to account for fullness. Taylor will consistently pose this as a question: whether one's ontology is adequate to support a sense of fullness. "Can you really give ontological space for these features short of admitting what you will want to deny, for instance, some reference to the transcendent, or to a larger cosmic force, or whatever? In other words is the intermediate position really viable?" (pp. 605-6).

For example, regarding our being moved by beauty — case 3 above: Can that "experience be made sense of in an ontology excluding the transcendent" (p. 606)? Taylor's answer is interesting: "Undoubtedly yes, but . . . only in part" (p. 607). Can the closed take account for the force of Bach or Dante or Chartres?[17] "Here the challenge is to the unbeliever, to find a non-theistic register in which to respond to them, *without impoverishment*" (p. 607). Or take another example from ethics (case 2 above): "what ontology do we need to make sense of our ethical or moral lives" (p. 608)? Can we account for moral agency within the confines of materialism? For example, can "a 'naturalist' account make sense of the phenomenology of universalism" (p. 609)?[18] This isn't an "account battle" that Taylor is trying to win, however; the point of these questions, at least in this context, is to displace the "spun" confidence of some "closed" accounts.

Remapping the Tensions; or, Dilemmas for Everyone

In the concluding sections of chapter 16, Taylor emphasizes that one of the central aspirations of modernity is the "aspiration to wholeness,"

---

17. Cp. Julian Barnes's discussion of religious art in *Nothing to Be Frightened Of* (London: Jonathan Cape, 2008).

18. Taylor takes this "step" in the nature of solidarity to be one of the "crucial features of modernity," one of modernity's key aspirations (p. 609).

which includes both an affirmation of ordinary life and an affirmation of the body and its desires. On the one hand, this was unleashed by the Reformation's recovery of a theology of creation that affirmed finitude, domestic life, and "secular$_1$" pursuits when undertaken *coram Deo;* on the other hand, something like this affirmation of the body and sensuality is often invoked as a *critique* of religion — as if religion were essentially "puritanical" or that religion "intrinsically and by its very nature frustrates this aspiration" (p. 618). So on the one hand it looks like religion is a *cause* for this affirmation of bodily "this-worldly" life; on the other hand, others claim religion is hostile to bodily life. A theology that affirms the goodness of creation would seem to affirm material life; but a theology fixated on heaven would seem to devalue it.

Taylor thinks both are true and tries to appreciate the complexity of issues here. On the one hand, he'll argue that behind this critique is a caricature of religion, and especially Christianity, which fails to appreciate the incarnational force of the Christian vision that *resists* excarnation (cp. p. 615).[19] On the other hand, he'll argue that, in fact, exclusive humanism has its own problems in this regard. In other words, there are enough dilemmas and internal tensions to go around; exclusive humanism is in no better position than Christianity on this front. In what follows, Taylor notes some shifts within modern Christianity and exclusive humanism that try to escape this tension.

From Sin to Sickness

Consider, for example, two very different ways to account for evil. If we're going to affirm ordinary life, then that needs to translate into some affirmation of the *goodness* of embodied, material life. But if we're going to talk about the goodness of ordinary life, we also need some account of what goes — or has gone — wrong, some account of evil and broken-

19. On this front, Taylor will tend to applaud and recommend "developments" and adaptations in contemporary Christianity that try to evade this critique. Here the critical reader needs to carefully sift Taylor's description from his prescriptions. While Taylor is sympathetic to historic, orthodox Christianity, he does not seem at all constrained by it and is willing to entertain revisions where I would not. But I will try to keep my polemics to a minimum, since my primary task is to lay out Taylor's argument.

ness. Taylor is interested in the significant cultural shifts in how we talk about this — from talking about sin to talking about sickness. These are two very different hermeneutics, two different ways of construing our current condition: the "spiritual"[20] versus the "therapeutic." "What was formerly sin is often now seen as sickness" (p. 618). The moral is transferred to a therapeutic register; in doing so we move from responsibility to victimhood.

As Taylor starkly puts it, in this therapeutic paradigm, there is no room for Lucifer: "The Lucifer story has no place in its aetiology" precisely because "there is no choice." What's wrong with me is more like a disease that befalls me than a disorder for which I am responsible. It's something from which I need to be healed, but on this therapeutic model, in contrast to ancient pictures, "healing doesn't involve conversion" (p. 619). "One reason to throw over the spiritual perspective evil/holiness was to reject the idea that our normal, middle-range existence is imperfect [essential to the 'spiritual' account]. We're perfectly all right as we are, as 'natural' beings. So the dignity of ordinary, 'natural' existence is even further enhanced." What would have been seen as vices are now construed as sickness; the one who exhibits melancholy is "one who is just incapacitated" and thus needs to be treated therapeutically — not one who has disordered love that needs to be rehabituated to charity. Indeed, on the therapeutic register, the spiritual is itself pathological, part of the problem that represses our nature.

There is a certain irony, however: while the therapeutic was meant to throw off the guilt and burden of spiritual responsibility, and hence the scowl of the clergy and confessor, "now we are forced to go to new experts, therapists, doctors, who exercise the kind of control that is appropriate over blind and compulsive mechanisms" (p. 620). In the name of securing our freedom, we swap submission to the priest for submission to the therapist.[21]

What Taylor thinks is lost in this therapeutic paradigm is precisely a sense that even our "normal, middle-range existence" is disordered and

20. The "spiritual" here corresponds to what he has earlier called a "transformationist" perspective.

21. Cp. Taylor's earlier discussion of those who reject faith "because of science," only to submit themselves to this new authority.

conflicted. The problem isn't just pathologies that beset our "normal" functioning — as if we could finally be liberated to be whole and healthy and happy if we just rid ourselves of the various "sicknesses" that beset us, *including religion.* No, according to the "spiritual" (transformationist) hermeneutic, even our best "normal" is going to be beset by tensions and unease. Our problem is not some penumbra of illness pressing in on our "good" normal; our problem *is* our "normal." On the spiritual register, "the 'normal,' everyday, beginning situation of the soul is to be partly in the grip of evil" (p. 619). "Hasn't Christian preaching always repeated that it is impossible to be fully happy as a sinful agent in a sinful world?" (p. 635) — something that much of contemporary Christianity would be surprised to hear. As Taylor observes, the "spiritual" perspective has room to recognize that "even people who are very successful in the range of normal human flourishing (perhaps especially such people) can feel unease, perhaps remorse, some sense that their achievements are hollow. From the perspective of those who deny this supposed spiritual reality, this unease can only be pathological; it is totally non-functional; it can only hold us back. The denial of much traditionally understood spiritual reality has been a crucial factor in the therapeutic turn" (p. 621). Indeed, on the spiritual account, it is precisely the transcendent that can mess you up; it's not that once you get your religious house in order and recognize the transcendent, all will be well.[22] To the contrary, it is precisely the push and pull of transcendence that create the dis-ease and uncanniness of our existence: "human beings are powerfully drawn to fullness under some or other definitions. And most people will concur that these aspirations can themselves be the source of deep troubles; for instance, strong moral demands can impact on our lives in the form of crippling guilt [welcome to Calvinism!]" (p. 622). This isn't because the spiritual befalls us as yet another pathology; rather, "from the spiritual perspective, that the demands of faith can produce crippling conflicts reflects not their gratuitous nature, but our real (fallen) predicament."

Now, it's not that there's no place for recognizing pathology (the "spiritual perspective" is not Scientology, and Taylor's not playing Tom Cruise

---

22. Indeed, at one point in *God Is the Bigger Elvis,* one of the novices recounts that Mother Prioress Dolores told her that the monastic life is "like being skinned alive."

to the therapist's Brooke Shields!). "The issue is whether one can speak of pathology alone" (p. 622). "The therapeutic revolution," Taylor concedes, "has brought a number of insights, approaches. It is just as a *total metaphysic* that it risks generating perverse results" (p. 623, emphasis added). There remains something in the "spiritual" or "transformationist" perspective that does justice to the cracks we feel in our existence — in ways that the exclusively humanist "therapeutic" construal can't make sense of.

Two Critiques of Religion

Let's return to the critique of Christianity generated by exclusive humanism's aspiration to wholeness — its affirmation of embodiment and all its attendant features (ordinary life, sexuality, etc.). Because it thinks only an immanentist perspective can truly include all that is material and natural and bodily, exclusive humanism sees the ascetic, disciplinary aspects of Christianity (and other religions) as denials and denigrations of "this-worldly" life. Taylor sees two different criticisms of Christianity generated by exclusive humanism on this score:

1. By inviting us to "transcend humanity," religion/Christianity actually mutilates us, asks us to repress what is really human (p. 623).

2. By holding out promises that the world could be otherwise, "religion tends to bowdlerize reality" — papering over the difficult aspects of nature (p. 624).

This two-pronged critique, or these parallel critiques, creates a dilemma: for Christianity, "it seems hard to avoid one of these criticisms without impaling oneself on the other." If you try to defend against the "repression" critique, you open yourself to the "bowdlerize" critique because you'll end up painting things as rosier than they are. But if you try to avoid pie-in-the-sky hopefulness (and thus avoid bowdlerizing our condition), you're going to sound awfully dour — in which case you're going to be newly subject to the repression critique.

The crucial turn in chapter 17 is when Taylor suggests that *exclusive humanism gets hung up on the same horns:* "one suspects that something similar may be true for unbelief. Unbelieving views may sell human beings short, in underestimating their ability to reform [the victimhood tendency above]; but they may also put the bar too high, and justify some very destructive attempts at change" (p. 624). Once again, the playing field is leveled here: it's not that Christianity faces a dilemma while exclusive humanism escapes the problem. Both are caught.

Taylor takes the example of Martha Nussbaum, who suggests that Christianity represents a repression of our humanness, a hubristic desire to transcend humanity by denying "natural" drives, passions, etc. (p. 626). But Taylor then asks: Doesn't Enlightenment humanism ask the same of us? Doesn't the "high bar" of Enlightenment "civilization" (and its attendant universalism) function *as* transcendence in this regard, asking us to repress some of our most human instincts and orientations? So is exclusive humanism really in any better position in this respect?

Immanent Counter-Enlightenment Redux

If Enlightenment humanism is itself a mode of "transcending" humanity, then it's not surprising to see in modernity a reaction to this *internal to immanence* — that is, reactions that have no interest in affirming transcendence but are nonetheless responding to the pressures of humanism. So, Taylor suggests, this is not simply a binary debate between belief and unbelief; it is a triangular debate between (1) secular humanists, (2) neo-Nietzschean antihumanists, and (3) "those who acknowledge some good beyond life" (p. 636).[23]

By complicating matters, Taylor helps us understand a curious phenomenon: that within the immanent frame, at times my enemy's enemy will be my friend. So acknowledgers of transcendence and exclusive humanists both affirm some kind of "transformation" that functions *as* a

---

23. Taylor later suggests that these might need to be separated into two different camps of "acknowledgers of transcendence": (a) those who see the whole move to humanism as a mistake that needs to be undone, and (b) those who appreciate modernity's emphasis on "the practical primacy of life" and recognize some good in the Enlightenment — who might even say "that modern unbelief is providential" (p. 637). Taylor places himself in the latter camp.

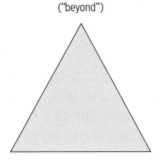

Acknowledgers of Transcendence
("beyond")

Exclusive humanists committed to
MMO (functions as a "beyond"
agape-analogue

neo-Nietzschean antihumanists
("will to power"; reject both
"beyond" *and* MMO)

Figure 4. Poles of the counter-Enlightenment

"beyond" to which humanity is called. As a result, while they have significant differences on one plane, vis-à-vis antihumanism they are united in their rejection of the will to power. Or if we slice the issues differently, the exclusive humanists and neo-Nietzscheans can be united in their rejection of specifically religious claims to transcendence. So if Martha Nussbaum and Nietzsche were in the same room, they would be locked in vociferous debate. But if Charles Taylor walked in and started talking about Christianity, Nussbaum and Nietzsche would forget their previous differences. As Taylor colorfully puts it: "Any pair can gang up against the third on some important issue" (p. 636). This triangulation picture might help us get a handle on why strange coalitions can arise in a secular age.

Which Christianity? The Maximal Demand

Let's return to the twofold critique of Christianity summarized above. It is said to be guilty of either "bowdlerizing" reality and papering over the difficulties of the human predicament *or* "mutilating" ordinary human (bodily) desires for the sake of some "beyond." This creates a dilemma since fending off one of the critiques seems to impale one on the horn of the other. Taylor summarizes the "dilemma" of what he'll call the "**maximal demand**": "how to define our highest spiritual or moral aspirations for human beings, while showing a path to the transformation involved which doesn't crush, mutilate or deny what is essential to our humanity" (pp. 639-40).

The maximal demand is (almost?) impossible to meet, so it might seem that "we either have to scale down our moral aspirations in order to allow our ordinary human life to flourish; or we have to agree to sacrifice some of this ordinary flourishing to secure our highest ideals" (p. 640). However, let's remember: this isn't just a problem for Christianity. Exclusive humanism probably faces the same dilemma, since the modern moral order of mutual benefit also sets up a moral aspiration that requires repressing, even "mutilating," ordinary human desires and bodily instincts: "Their highest aspirations too run the risk of mortifying ordinary human life. They hide this from themselves, either because they under-rate how far we are from their goal — they underestimate human depravity, to use the traditional language — and so deserve the bowdlerizing reproach (think of Niebuhr's critique of liberalism); or they are cavalier about the costs of reaching the goal, and hence deserve the mortifying reproach" (p. 641).[24]

In some sense, the challenge is actually intensified for exclusive humanism, precisely because it can only admit the immanent: if the maximal demand is going to be met, it has to be met *by us* and in "the here and now" (or at least within "secular" time). And if we *don't* reach it, we have only ourselves to blame. Christianity, on the other hand, can be ambivalent, or even a tad pessimistic about the maximal demand being realized by us in the here and now because the transformationist perspective is also eschatological. For Christianity, "this is a transformation which cannot be completed in history" (p. 643). This is why "Christians don't really 'have the solution' to the dilemma" either: because "the direction they point to cannot be *demonstrated* as right; it must be taken on faith"; and because "we can't exhibit fully what it means, lay it out in a code or a fully-specified life-form, but only point to the exemplary lives of certain

24. Taylor notes that one way out of the dilemma for the exclusive humanist is to reject the *universalism* of the Enlightenment (the Nietzschean option) (p. 642).

trail-blazing people and communities" (p. 643, emphasis added). You might say Christian eschatology buys time to meet the maximal demand — time exclusive humanism doesn't (can't) have.

However, we also need to recognize that some forms of Christianity are more guilty of "mutilation" than others — that some more egregiously fail the maximal demand. This leads Taylor to recognize that there are Christiani*ties,* but to also claim that "there are clearly *wrong* versions of Christian faith" (p. 643). Here he is clearly moving from the descriptive to the normative, laying out several "misprisions" of Christianity. What's not always clear is the source for his *criteria* by which forms of Christianity are judged to be wrong. As I noted above, Taylor seems willing to jettison aspects of historic Christian teaching if he thinks doing so will help meet the maximal demand. Others (such as myself) would press for more imaginative ways to consider retaining the historic Christian teaching while also noting the pressures of the maximal demand. Ultimately that might require calling into question the presuppositions that underwrite this maximal demand in the first place, in particular the *anthropocentrism* of the demand, which is fixated on expectations of human flourishing — an anthropocentrism that Taylor seems to uncritically accept.

"Platonizing" Christianities

He first considers "Platonizing" renditions of Christianity — excarnating forms that denigrate embodiment (and hence the forms most susceptible to Nietzschean critique).[25] Thus the question, as Taylor sees it, is this: "How can Christians speak of transformation without becoming closet Platonists?" (p. 644). "Authentic" (i.e., nonmisprisioned!) Christianity will be incarnational, and thus should not so easily fall prey to the "repression" or "mutilating" critique — though not even such an authentic, incarnational Christian fully escapes the dilemma.

Another (still Platonizing) "wrong" form of Christianity misunderstands the nature of ascetic sacrifice. In this misprision, what is sacri-

---

25. However, there can also be deistic misprisions that are guilty of giving up the transformationism of "authentic" Christianity.

ficed is castigated as bad, whereas in authentic Christianity, the sacrifice *is* a sacrifice precisely because what's "given up" is not essentially bad or evil. It is *not* a "constitutive incompatibility" (p. 645) but rather a temporal, existential tension. The transformationist perspective does not *essentially* denigrate what's sacrificed, but rather *strategically.* It is characterized by a "fundamental ambivalence."[26] This will always sit in tension with an immanentist move that is not haunted by any "beyond" that would ever *ask* for ascetic denial. And this immanentization — in which ascetic denial makes no sense — will be part of what cross-pressures faith in a secular age.[27] Here Taylor tends to focus on sex.[28] So, for example, transformationist Christianity emphasized the importance of chastity and celebrated celibacy as a calling. This obviously curtails bodily desires and cravings, "repressing" sexual urges, etc. Does it thereby denigrate sex as evil? Not necessarily. It only relativizes the good of sex vis-à-vis other (eternal) goods, asking us to sacrifice a relative good to achieve an ultimate good. But in "Platonizing" forms, the sex that is denied and repressed is not really a "sacrifice" but more an evil that is exorcised. So we have two very different "Christiani*ties*" at work here. The misprision of the "Platonic" form is rightly criticized (and rejected), but the non-Platonic version is actually trying to manage the tension of the maximal demand.

Punishment and "Modern Christian Consciousness"
(or, "Rob Bell, Meet Charles Taylor")

Christianity is "transformationist" precisely because it posits a *redemption,* a *salvation;* "and salvation points to the possibility of damnation, and hence of divine punishment" (p. 646). However, it is precisely this

---

26. I think this is what is increasingly being lost in (Kuyperianized) American Christianity. Cp. Hans Boersma, *Heavenly Participation: The Weaving of a Sacramental Tapestry* (Grand Rapids: Eerdmans, 2010).

27. Consider again *God Is the Bigger Elvis.*

28. "I think that there is a real tension involved in trying to combine in one life sexual fulfillment and piety" (p. 645). Is this because he's unwittingly and uncritically accepting some notion of "sexual fulfillment"? Cp. David Matzko McCarthy, *Sex and Love in the Home: A Theology of the Household* (London: SCM, 2004).

doctrine of damnation and divine punishment that is especially suscepti-ble to the repression or "mutilating" critique: eternal punishment would be the ultimate "repression" of ordinary human fulfillment. So for the ex-clusive humanist, "all religion is ultimately Moloch drinking blood from the skulls of the slain. The Old Testament critique of the Phoenician cults is now extended to faith in the transcendent as such" (p. 648). This is an especially vexing problem for Christianities that affirm that "God not only wills our good, a good which includes human flourishing, but was willing to go to extraordinary lengths to ensure this, in the becoming human and suffering of his son" (p. 649). Indeed, if one makes the "anthropo-logical turn" and begins to affirm that *all*[29] God really cares about is *our* flourishing, then aspects of Christianity begin to look untenable: "If the good that God wills for us doesn't just include, *but consists entirely* in human flourishing, what sense does it make to sacrifice some part of this in order to serve God?" Sacrifice becomes untenable, even unthinkable (hence the rejection of traditional theories of the atonement). There is no room left in our plausibility structures to make sense of divine violence — which again undercuts any notion of "atonement" (p. 649). Indeed, the penal substitutionary account of the atonement can only look "mon-strous." Which is why the cross drops out; what becomes important is the *life* of Christ — what he says or teaches (p. 650). We're on our way to Unitarianism.

"So in this anthropocentric climate, where we keep any idea of the spiritual, it must be totally constructive, positive. . . . The wrath of God disappears, leaving only His love" (p. 649). And so we get "the striking modern phenomenon": "the decline of Hell" (p. 650). Enter Rob Bell.[30]

So shouldn't an "authentic" Christianity want to turn back the clock? "Isn't the answer easy? Just undo the anthropocentric turn" (p. 651). Not so fast, cautions Taylor. First, even if we wanted to, there's no simplistic going back. The anthropocentric turn is in the water; it's increasingly the

29. This is what makes Jonathan Edwards not only unthinkable but reprehensible to modern sensibilities: Edwards's God is *about God,* not us.

30. See Rob Bell, *Love Wins: A Book about Heaven, Hell, and the Fate of Every Person Who Ever Lived* (San Francisco: HarperOne, 2011). See also Kelefa Sanneh's profile of Bell, "The Hell-Raiser: A Megachurch Pastor's Search for a More Forgiving Faith," *New Yorker,* November 26, 2012, pp. 56-65.

air we breathe.[31] Not even orthodox Christians might realize the extent to which we've absorbed this by osmosis. Second, for Taylor, we shouldn't want to.[32] Taylor attributes this whole atonement-damnation complex to a "hyper-Augustinianism" that assumed that "the majority of the human race will be damned" (p. 652), and this is clearly an aspect of the tradition with which he does not want to be associated.[33] But, he claims, "there is also a broader band of Christian belief and sensibility for which the decline of Hell is a positive change" (p. 653). So we get "modern Christian consciousness" (p. 655).

> This modern Christian consciousness thus lives in a tension, that may feel at times like a dilemma, between what it draws from the development of modern humanism, and its attachment to the central mysteries of Christian faith. It endorses the decline of Hell, the rejection of the juridical-penal model of the atonement, and any hermeneutic of divine violence, as well as affirming the full value of human flourishing. But it cannot accept the self-enclosure in immanence, and is aware that God has given a new transformative meaning to suffering and death in the life and death of Christ. (pp. 655-56)

But it's hard to see how this isn't — or isn't on the way to — a new deism. At this point in the argument, we seem to be getting Taylor's tastes and preferences, with little warrant beyond that. One could raise a number of questions in this regard: Are we evaluating "misprisions" here by some kind of *vote,* as if this were a democratic process by which we determine what Christians ought to believe by seeing what the majority consider acceptable? Surely being "hard to believe" (pp. 654-55) is not a sufficient cri-

31. This could be true without being deterministic. In a similar way, Taylor emphasizes that there's no way to now get out of the "immanent frame." Nonetheless, one can affirm transcendence *within* the immanent frame. Similarly, I would suggest, we could come to a recognition of the ubiquity of the anthropocentric Zeitgeist but from within that affirm the plausibility of a radically theo-centric imaginary. I think this is just what we find in the renewed interest in Augustine and Jonathan Edwards.

32. Here I find Taylor frustrating and idiosyncratic. Why affirm *this* aspect of the anthropocentric turn? It seems ad hoc inconsistent to me — and just the result of the fact that Taylor doesn't want to be associated with the implications of consistency on this score.

33. Is the problem that a *majority* will be damned? Or that *any* will?

terion — if it were, then Taylor's whole account of transcendence would be dismissed because it's "hard to believe" for many exclusive humanists. What's coming home to roost is something we noted earlier: Taylor's (unstated) criteria for judging what counts as a misprision.

What about Violence?

Let's turn to a version of the repression or "mutilating" critique that is basically Freudian in spirit, but also reflected in recent discussions in evolutionary psychology (and hence important as Christians grapple with the implications of evolutionary accounts of human origins). The question put to Christianity (the featured "acknowledger of transcendence" in figure 4) is this: Can you account for what seem to be essentially human *"drives"* (desire, sexuality, violence, etc.), features of humanity that seem to be simply *natural?* Does the "transformationism" of Christianity essentially "mutilate" and repress basic features of being human? And therefore isn't Christianity essentially an antihumanism?

We've seen Taylor's tack in response to the repression critique: (1) Well, I'm not sure Enlightenment humanism escapes the same problems and (2) I can imagine a rendition of Christianity that is something like a "humanism with transcendence." In that same vein, then, Taylor addresses what seems to be a "natural" human drive toward *violence* (again, compare Freud's account of Thanatos in *Civilization and Its Discontents*).[34]

On the one hand, it might seem that Christianity has an easy answer to hand: violence is not "natural," it is a reflection of *depravity* (p. 657). However, the "modern Christian consciousness" he has just articulated (p. 655) is less inclined to this answer because it "sees how inextricably interwoven human self-affirmation is with its distorted forms" (p. 657).[35] In particular, it is challenged and puzzled by "frenzied" violence, the wild side of human nature that seems to especially manifest itself in young men. How are we to account for this? "What to make of this?"

---

34. This would add ammunition to Taylor's point re: Enlightenment humanism: on Freud's account, "civilization" is essentially a repression, a mutilation.

35. Of course, an Augustinian account of "depravity" can recognize the same, but I won't dwell on that point here.

"One common approach in our culture is the disengaged, objectifying 'scientific' one. The propensity to violence can be understood in biological, evolutionary terms. It is in some ways 'wired into' us" (p. 657). If one takes this route, then irruptions of violence are evolutionary throwbacks: "culture evolves, and brings higher and higher standards of moral behaviour. We now live with and partly by, notions of human rights which are incomparably more demanding than in previous civilizations; but the old drives lurk there still, waiting for certain extreme conditions which will allow them to break out" (p. 658). And so the impulsion to violence cannot be effaced from our genes or our hormones or what have you.

But for Taylor, "this seems radically insufficient. It's not that body chemistry is not a crucial factor, but that it never operates alone in human life, but only through the meanings that things have for us. The hormonal explanation doesn't tell us why people are susceptible to certain *meanings*" (p. 659, emphasis added). So the merely biological account is insufficient; we need a "meta-biological" account, a *cultural* account that explains how violence *means* in our secular age. If a purely biological account is what's left to us in a "closed" take, then Taylor is scoring an apologetic point: maybe a "closed" take doesn't really have the resources to make sense of our secular age; and maybe that opens the door for a closer consideration of an "open" take.

Taylor thinks it is "obvious" that "Christianity requires some kind of meta-biological account of our impulsions to violence" (p. 660). However, before getting there, he considers another option: the Nietzschean celebration of and affirmation of these impulses to violence. The representative here is Bataille (pp. 661-64).[36] The upshot of this "take" is not just a recognition of the inescapability of violence but its ritual celebration and channeling: "The attempts to train humans out of it, leave it behind us in the disciplines of civilization, are not only bound to fail, but also represent a mutilation of human life" (p. 664). Once again, we see how the

---

36. Or some other "post-Schopenhauerian vision of things." On this take, "that humans inflict pain and suffering on others is part of the very way of things, the way the dark and inhuman universe resonates in us. To see this is to intuit the *tragedy* at the basis of human life" (p. 664, emphasis added). Representatives here include Hemingway and the poet Robinson Jeffers (pp. 665-67).

antihumanist critique falls on both Christianity's transcendence and the Enlightenment's "civilization" (Nussbaum's "internal transcendence").

Taylor retools the question slightly when he gets to Christianity: "whether the propensity to violence is biological or metaphysical, this still leaves an enigma that any Christian understanding must explain: how can human nature *as we know it* be in the image of God?" (p. 668, emphasis added). In response, he offers a hypothesis: sure, he says, "humans are born out of the animal kingdom," so it's no surprise that they (especially males) exhibit "a powerful sex-drive, and lots of aggression." But they are also created *to be guided by God.* "Being guided by God means some kind of transformation *of* these drives; not just their repression, or suppression, keeping the lid on them; but some real turning of them from within, conversion, so that all the energy now goes along with God." Eros will fuel agape; aggression becomes the energy to combat evil. What, then, *is* "evil" in such a hypothesis? It is a resistance to the education of our desires by God — a resistance to the call to be transformed.

Now, on the one hand, this pedagogy feels a tad Pelagian;[37] or rather, it feels merely "progressive" and rather deistic: "God is slowly educating mankind, slowly turning it, transforming it from within" (p. 668). There is little space in this model for the cross (cp. p. 673). On the other hand, Taylor also qualifies the picture: "there can and must also be leaps. Otherwise no significant forward steps will be made in the response to God. Someone has to break altogether with some historic forms. Abraham is our paradigm for this" (p. 669). At first it might seem that the "leap" here is from below: Abraham is a *hero,* an overcomer. But in the next paragraph there is a hint that the leap is generated by downward force, akin to grace: it is "the revelation to Abraham" that makes the difference. "And with revelation comes a gift of *power*" (p. 669, emphasis added). There is then a further revelation with Christ, which brings a new gift of power. Why Taylor avoids the traditional language of "grace" here is not clear.

Christianity, then, in contrast to both the naturalization thesis and the neo-Nietzschean celebration, does not think that violence is ineradicable, "too deeply anchored to be rooted out" (p. 672). However, that doesn't

---

37. Note Taylor's earlier comments on cultural "Pelagianisms" of various stripes.

let Christianity off the hook, either: we are still pressed by a dilemma, namely, how things could be this bad, especially if you recognize/concede that these are in fact responses to divine pedagogy. This should lead us to recognize "a fundamental ambivalence of human reality" (p. 673). So once again, both exclusive humanism and Christianity are hooked on the same horns. That shouldn't be cause for premature rejoicing for Christians (p. 674), since that would just be Schadenfreude — we don't have a "solution" either (p. 675). Instead, it raises the apologetic question: "who can respond most profoundly and convincingly to what are ultimately commonly felt dilemmas?" (p. 675). The secular$_3$ age is a level playing field. We're all trying to make sense of where we are, even *why* we are, and it's not easy for any of us.

That is about the extent of Taylor's "apologetics." First, level the playing field (for example, by pointing out that both exclusive humanism and Christianity face dilemmas); second, show some of the inadequacy of purely "immanentist" accounts, opening space for a Christian account to receive a hearing; and then, third, sketch how a Christian "take" might offer a more nuanced or more comprehensive account of our experience (a phenomenological strategy).[38]

Taylor insists that, while he believes a Christian "take" can account for aspects of our experience that an exclusively humanist "take" cannot, he is not primarily interested in winning an argument. Rather, his concern is to foster a "badly needed" conversation. **How might evangelism and outreach in a secular$_3$ age be considered a form of just such a "conversation"? Could unapologetic "witnessing" also involve attentive "listening"?**

Some have been critical of Taylor's apologetic strategy, as if *A Secular Age* was a covert Christian tract masquerading under the

---

38. This sort of strategy is akin to the school of thought described as "Reformed epistemology," associated with Alvin Plantinga and Nicholas Wolterstorff. Some have said that Reformed epistemology offers a "negative apologetic": rather than offering a demonstration or "proofs" for Christianity, the Reformed epistemologist instead seeks to show that Christian faith is warranted and thus cannot be written off as irrational. Such faith has the same epistemic footing as all sorts of other beliefs — a "leveling-the-playing-field" strategy akin to some of Taylor's moves. For a helpful discussion, see Deane-Peter Baker, *Tayloring Reformed Epistemology: Charles Taylor, Alvin Plantinga, and the* De Jure *Challenge to Christian Belief* (London: SCM, 2007).

guise of a "neutral" analysis.[39] Taylor's retort is twofold: first, *no one* can offer an account that is "take"-free, so to speak. Second, though he is unapologetic about his own commitments, he doesn't think his Catholic faith precludes the analysis having wider purchase. So, he'll say, "I suppose that I'm offering reasons for a certain kind of Christian position,"[40] and "in the interests of full disclosure," he admits, "I am happy to state where I personally stand." But then he immediately adds: *"But this is not the conclusion of the book."*[41] He continues:

> This is not what I'm trying to do. If the book has a desired perlocutionary effect, it is rather this: I think what we badly need is a conversation between a host of different positions, religious, nonreligious, antireligious, humanistic, antihumanistic, and so on, in which we eschew mutual caricature and try to understand what "fullness" means for the other. What makes me impatient are the positions that are put forward as conversation-stoppers: I have a three-line argument which shows that your position is absurd or impossible or totally immoral. Of course, I have my own, theologically defined reasons for wanting this, but I also know that we can have a widely based "overlapping consensus" on the value of this conversation.[42]

So his unapologetic starting point doesn't preclude shared conversation *in* the cross-pressured space of the secular. But neither does that preclude participants from making a case for their "take." The remainder of his argument tends to operate in this mode.

---

39. See, for example, Jonathan Sheehan, "When Was Disenchantment? History and the Secular Age," in *Varieties of Secularism in a Secular Age,* ed. Michael Warner, Jonathan VanAntwerpen, and Craig Calhoun (Cambridge: Harvard University Press, 2010), pp. 217-42, and Martin Jay, "Faith-Based History," *History and Theory* 48 (2009): 76-84.

40. Taylor, afterword in *Varieties of Secularism in a Secular Age,* p. 320.

41. Taylor, afterword in *Varieties of Secularism in a Secular Age,* p. 318, emphasis in original.

42. Taylor, afterword in *Varieties of Secularism in a Secular Age,* p. 318. He goes on to say that, admittedly, it is his Catholic faith that motivates his desire for just this cross-"take" conversation (pp. 319-20).

What Does It All Mean?

Following Luc Ferry, Taylor suggests that our secular age is cross-pressured with respect to *meaning* — or more specifically, the "meaning of meaning." It's not something we can easily escape precisely because "what we do always has a point; we undertake various projects, and in-between we keep going the routines which sustain our lives" (p. 677). There is an inherent teleology in our actions, and one that seems to always implicitly have an "ultimate" to which it is aimed, even if we so often concern ourselves with the penultimate. So there is always a "meta-question" to be asked, and that will haunt us — sometimes especially when it seems that "significance" should be most clear: "What is the meaning of it all?"

There can be different responses to the force of this question. "Some people hold that one shouldn't ask this meta-question, that one should train oneself not to feel the need." However, it's also not easily suppressed, and "once it arises for someone they will not easily be put off by the injunction to forget it." It's like being told to *not* think of pink flying elephants. This nasty existential genie cannot be easily put back in the bottle. Indeed, Taylor is suspicious of those exclusive humanism accounts that want to just squelch this question — a question that "arises out of a sense that there are goals which could engage us more fully and deeply than our ordinary ends," a "sense" that "somewhere there is a fullness or richness which transcends the ordinary." "This," Taylor cautions, "will not easily be uprooted from the human heart" (p. 677).

A "more effective" response is immanentizing rather than suppressing, offering an answer that is "within the natural-human domain," offering "a kind of transcendence of our ordinary existence" — a "horizontal transcendence" akin to Nussbaum's "internal transcendence" (p. 677). This is basically to treat the modern moral order (MMO) *as if* it were transcendent. As we'll see below, however, Taylor wonders whether this horizontal transcendence can bear the weight of what's needed — whether it is an adequate "ontology" (recall the discussion above). Is it a sufficient load-bearing beam for our ethical predicament, or even what exclusive humanism wants?

The reductionist — the "closed spinner," that is — has his own account of why people "go religious": it's because they are "looking for meaning." The closed spinner offers a "general theory of religious motivations" that "explains" religious responses in terms of something other than religion (thus explaining religion away).

But Taylor is skeptical of both the very possibility of such a general theory and the specific accounts given for "what humans seek in religion." It's *not* "meaning," and it's certainly not meaning in general, he says. "Indeed, there is something absurd about the idea that our lives could be focused on meaning as such, rather than on some specific good or value. One might die for God, or the Revolution, or the classless society, but not for meaning" (p. 679). Only an already secularist$_2$ "theory" of religion would suggest this. But "anyone genuinely 'into' some good or value must see this particular good as having worth; this is what he is moved by" (p. 680).

So what *does* motivate our spiritual commitments, if it's not "meaning in general"? What *are* the specific goods or values we are pursuing in our spiritual lives? Taylor's move here is interesting. Per his own account of the "triangulation" that can happen in the immanent frame, one might say that Taylor teams up with Nietzsche here in order to "gang up on" exclusive humanism's reductionism.

Whence religious belief and spiritual motivations? Well, perhaps it begins with a common experience: we become overwhelmed by evil and suffering. Though we live in a disenchanted world, we can once again feel "unprotected": "now not from demons and spirits, but from suffering and evil as we sense it raging in the world" (p. 681). This can generate a couple of different responses:

a. A *negative,* self-defensive response that tries to just shut this all out — to cancel the horror by turning off the news, distracting ourselves incessantly, or making ourselves numb so that we can forget that anything's wrong (clearly guilty of the bowdlerizing charge).

b. A *positive* response: do something to heal the world, *tikkun olam,* be part of the solution (at least).

But then the question is: How effective are these strategies? "How much do we cope with the sense of the world's misery by the various defensive, exclusionary moves, and how much by the practices of tikkun?" (p. 682). Well, both seem to involve a certain *distancing* that is intrinsic to "the modern disengaged stance." However, this can take several different forms:

1. *Liberal distance:* you act compassionately, but with limits. You don't let yourself be overwhelmed by it. You're engaged in amelioration, *tikkun,* but let's not get crazy: you still want to enjoy a good bottle of wine and want to be able to sleep at night. This is the response of David Brooks's *Bobos in Paradise* or the liberal do-gooders in Franzen's *Freedom.*

2. *Bolshevik distance:* Here you also are confidently engaged in amelioration, being part of the solution, but you are also very confident of the trajectory and strategy, and thus are willing to be a hard-ass about it, to make the hard decisions. "All benevolence is now invested in this all-powerful ameliorative action; so that what is out of reach of this can be sacrificed, ruthlessly set aside. This allows one to be brutal, to transgress principles of universal respect for innocent human life; and this in a way that liberalism cannot follow, where the sense of our limitation enforces negative checks" (p. 682). This can get to the point where you abandon commitment to universal benefit: "Here the first positive part of the answer is no longer benevolence, but the idea that the human type demands realization of its excellence, and only the few can do this; so they must go ahead" (p. 683). Kind of fascist *tikkun olam,* but with the best of intentions.

3. *The victim scenario* (a tendency of the Left): "All evil is projected onto the others; they alone are the victimizers; we are pure victim" (p. 683). This amounts to "a kind of deviant, secularized Christianity" that achieves a pure martyrdom — it "achieves total innocence, at the cost of projecting evil on the other" (p. 684). The problem is, this can generate its own "Bolshevik-type ruthlessness."

On one level, Taylor is engaged in another exercise in leveling the playing field; it turns out that it's not just belief in transcendence that can engender violence as a response to evil. Humanisms of various stripes, even those committed to amelioration, can engender their own violent responses to evil. On another level, however, Taylor is not content to just level the playing field. He also suggests that, in fact, once you level the playing field, you might also notice that exclusive humanism has certain disadvantages: "Then the question may arise whether any humanistic view, just because it is woven around a picture of the potential greatness of human beings, doesn't tempt us to neglect the failures, the black-guards, the useless, the dying, those on the way out, in brief, those who negate the promise. Perhaps only God, and to some extent those who connect themselves to God, can love human beings when they are utterly abject" (p. 685). This "points to a purified Christian alternative, where one could aim to dwell in the suffering and evil without recoil, sure of the power of God to transform it." But this is not an "activist" response, precisely because it is fundamentally ambivalent about the prospects of transformation apart from God's grace. On this picture, "one is part of the solution by being there and praying, being there and affirming the good which is never absent" (p. 685). It lacks any of the Pelagian activism that would expect success; but as a result, Taylor hints, it might actually be *less dangerous* than well-intentioned *tikkun* of various forms.

Indeed, there is a curious (and worrisome) *confidence* that marks exclusive humanism: "Our whole view of ourselves," Taylor observes, "based on our modern understanding of morality, and an ordered, disci-plined society of mutual benefit, is that we have moved (in some favoured countries), and are moving (in less favoured ones) to a civilization which entrenches democracy and human rights." But *"what is the basis of this confident prospect?"* (p. 691, emphasis added). Whence our optimism? Is there any adequate basis for this (over)confidence?

It's not enough to simply count on "human nature." "It seems we need a stronger ethic, a firmer identification with the common good, more solidarity, if we are really to enter the promised land of a self-sustaining ethical code, or even meet the basic condition of the modern moral order, that our interaction really be of mutual benefit" (p. 692). The problem is that all sorts of secular solidarities generate violence (nationalism, etc.).

This raises the question of *motivation* for exclusive humanism: "the motivation which underlies our highest aspirations" (p. 693). Taylor is going to describe this as our "moral source."[43] But identifying our moral *sources* is not the same as providing an explanation of our moral responses. To identify our moral sources is to get at what *moves* us, what draws out of us this kind of action. What would it take to sufficiently *motivate* universal sympathy?

For example, the MMO is supposed to be motivated by our recognition of the *dignity* of human others (p. 694). The question will be: Is that an *adequate* moral source (p. 695; cp. pp. 605-6)? The MMO asks a lot of us: "Our age makes higher demands of solidarity and benevolence on people today than ever before. Never before have people been asked to stretch out so far, and so consistently, so systematically, so as a matter of course, to the stranger outside the gates" (p. 695). How do we manage to do it? Or how *could* we?

"Well, one way is that performance of these standards has become part of what we understand as a decent, civilized human life" (p. 696). The mechanism then becomes *shame:* to not meet these expectations is not only to be abnormal but almost inhuman. One can see this at work in a heightened version of holier-than-Thou: You don't recycle (gasp)? You use plastic shopping bags (horror)? You don't drive a Prius (eek!)? "You won't wear the ribbon?!"[44] This has to also be seen in light of Taylor's earlier analysis of the sociality of *mutual display* and the self-consciousness it generates (pp. 481-82). So what we get is justice *chic*.

However, this kind of self-congratulating, enlightened concern for the other is also susceptible to fatigue (p. 696): "Before the reality of human shortcomings, philanthropy — the love of the human — can gradually come to be invested with contempt, hatred, aggression" (p. 697). While I'm motivated to help the poor and vulnerable and even the undeserving because of their inherent dignity, I'm at the same time quietly patting myself on the back, recognizing my moral superiority. So over time it becomes frustrating that these other humans do not exhibit the same enlightened other-regard: *What's wrong with these people?*[45] "The tragic irony is that the higher the sense of potential, the more grievously real

---

43. Here, once again, he returns to terrain that was central in *Sources of the Self*.

44. Alluding to a classic episode of *Seinfeld*.

45. This is a dynamic explored well in both Walter's and Patty's character in Franzen's *Freedom*.

people fall short, and the more severe the turn-around will be which is inspired by the disappointment" (p. 697). It's not long before "you become the monster, so the monster will not break you" (U2). Your philanthropy becomes misanthropy.[46]

But of course, now you've played right into the hands of the Nietzschean critique: I *knew* it, he'll gloat. Behind all your pity and compassion has been a secret loathing. And all this philanthropy has really been self-interest and self-congratulation. "A Nietzschean genealogist can have a field day here" (p. 698).

"Perhaps after all, it's safer to have small goals, not too great expectations, be somewhat cynical about human potentiality from the start" (p. 699). And Taylor hints that acknowledging transcendence can actually relativize our expectations, thus guarding us against this fatigue, frustration, and inevitable misanthropy. So once again a subtle suggestion: maybe Christianity is less dangerous than liberalism.

Taylor finishes on something of an apologetic note, pointing out a possible superiority of the Christian "take." If you don't think agape is a real possibility, and if you've sort of conceded to a basic Hobbesian war of all with all, and if you don't think there is a God or grace or transformation, "then it may appear that the awe-inspiring, Stoic courage of a Camus or a Derrida must be our highest aspiration" (p. 703). But if you think a loving response to others as the image of God is *really* possible — if you think there is (or just might be) a God — then your entire picture of our ethical predicament has to be different. Here Taylor lays his cards on the table: "I think this can be real for us, but only to the extent that we open ourselves to God, which means in fact, overstepping the limits set in theory by exclusive humanisms. If one does believe that, then one has something very important to say to modern times, something that addresses the fragility of what all of us, believer and unbeliever alike, most value in these times" (p. 703). Taylor seems to be suggesting that we are the recipients of our own self-fulfilling prophecies; deciding beforehand that exclusive humanism sets the conditions for our moral life, we have thereby *shut down our openness to transformation.*

46. Note the allusion to Schopenhauer; for Schopenhauer, the crime is not being born, it's giving birth (p. 699). Now compare this to the references to Schopenhauer by the staid Midwestern father in Franzen's novel *The Corrections.*

Sites of Unease; or, The Restlessness
of Exclusive Humanism

The final section of chapter 18 takes up this question of moral *sources* in terms of moral *motivation*. The MMO significantly ramps up our moral *expectations;* indeed, we've gone beyond the Smithian vision of self-interest benefiting the whole. In a real sense, the MMO is a high calling to altruism and other-regard. However, because of an inadequate appreciation for moral *sources,* modernity fixates on moral *articulation* — a fixation on more and more scrupulous *codes* of behavior that further and further delineate high moral expectations (p. 703). Thus "a great deal of effort in modern liberal society is invested in defining and applying codes of conduct" (p. 704). Policy is driven by a kind of "code fixation": we don't know how to *make* people moral, but we do know how to specify rules, articulate expectation, lay down the law. This happens in policy but also informally in cultural codes of "political correctness" or even the unspoken codes of the Mommy-and-me play group.[47]

What's wrong with such code fixation? Well, on the one hand, there are all kinds of epistemological limitations: no code can anticipate every vagary of circumstance; no one can adequately know how to apply codes to new situations; we're not sure what to do when codes conflict; etc. These are all epistemological concerns that see the problem as one of *knowledge* (or lack thereof).

But there is also a more radical critique of such code fixation that Taylor's really after: codes don't make people care for their neighbor. In other words, codes are inadequate *as moral sources* precisely because they do not touch on the dynamics of moral motivation. It was not a code or a rule that produced forgiveness in Nelson Mandela. This points up precisely what's missing in modern moral philosophy: attention to motivation. "For clearly moving higher in the dimension of reconciliation and trust involves a kind of motivational conversion" (p. 707) — and no code can bring that about. So the "nomolatry" and "code fetishism" of modern

47. Philosophical ethics in modernity displays the same deontological code fixation; while there are all sorts of bombastic debates between Kantians and utilitarians, in fact they're all agreed that ethics comes down to specifying a *rule* (p. 704).

liberal society are an inadequate *source* for morality. In other words, modernity can't have what it wants on its own terms.[48]

So we bump up against the radical incompleteness of the MMO. Does that mean "religion" can sweep in and save the day? No, says Taylor. "Both sides have the virus" (p. 709). In other words, "we are all to blame." So once again, it's not a matter of pitting the religious against exclusive humanism, but first pointing out that both are pressed — cross-pressured — in the same way. But, as we've noted already, Taylor's strategy is cagey: on the one hand, he wants to level the playing field. On the other hand, once he's leveled the playing field, he'll begin to question the adequacy of the exclusive humanist immanentist account — not to "prove" Christianity true, but to make it at least more plausible. That then becomes a central task of chapter 19.

Taylor presses the closed, immanentist "take" not by pointing out logical inconsistencies or questioning the veracity of premises, but rather by suggesting that the closed take can't seem to get rid of a certain haunting, a certain rumbling in our hearts. There is a specter haunting our secular age, "the spectre of meaninglessness" (p. 717) — which is, in a sense, a dispatch from fullness. And because this won't go away, but rather keeps pressing and pulling, it generates "unease" (p. 711) and "restlessness" (p. 726). The upshot will be that Christianity (the "open" take) can provide a better way to account for this — not necessarily a way to quell it so we can all live happily ever after, but a way to *name* it and be honest about this dis-ease.

This unease and restlessness manifests itself in two domains of modern experience: time and death.

a. Time

We have already seen how modernity does away with "higher" times, leaving us to the merely chronological tick-tock of "secular" time. However, our own experience suggests that the unstoppable homogeneity of time

---

48. This is very analogous to Eric Gregory's critique of modern liberalism for neglecting "perfectionism" — the matter of moral formation. See Gregory, *Politics and the Order of Love: An Augustinian Ethic of Democratic Citizenship* (Chicago: University of Chicago Press, 2008).

is unbearable and unsustainable for us as humans. "It is doubtful if humans could ever live exclusively in this" (p. 714). There are two ways that we shape time, and thereby give shape to our world: cycles and narratives.

"Time for us continues to be marked by cycles, through which we orient ourselves." This creates rhythms of intensity and rest, but also creates a frame to help constitute our world and our experience. So rhythms, routines, and cycles of time *make* the world for us and thus delineate significance. This can be as simple as the regular routines of the workday and the "festival" of "the weekend." It might be as mundane as "spring cleanup" and "summer vacation." Or it can include the rites of passage of graduation, going to college, getting married, etc. These routines frame our lives, "distinguishing different moments from each other, giving each its sense, creating mini-kairoi to mark the passage of time. It's as though we humans have a need for gathered time, in one form or another."

We also "gather" time in narrative and story. We organize our own identities in an implicit (or sometimes explicit) autobiographical narrative (p. 714).[49] But "we" also create *national* stories — the story of our (modern) tribe that we narrate over and over again. Indeed, public *commemoration* gathers time both in a cycle of observance/remembrance *and* in the form of a compressed, performed narrative (p. 715).

But both of these strategies are destabilized and fragilized by "the spectre of meaninglessness." For while these might be intended to function *like* the rituals and narratives of premodern "higher" time, in fact we can be visited by the fear/realization that we're just making this up — that we're papering over an abyss. Thus what threatens the supposed self-sufficiency of our "timekeeping" is vapidity — meaninglessness does not manifest itself as fear but as *boredom* — or perhaps the fear *of* boredom.[50] "In earlier years, it would have seemed bizarre to fear an absence of meaning. When humans were posed between salvation and damnation, one might protest at the injustice and cru-

49. Taylor here links the rise of the genre of the memoir to this timekeeping function. That might be partly true, but I think the explosion of the memoir today is better linked to his earlier discussion of mutual display.

50. This, of course, was the central concern of David Foster Wallace's unfinished novel, published as *The Pale King* (New York: Little, Brown, 2010).

elty of an avenging God, but not that there were no important issues left" (p. 717). Tedium and ennui are the demons of modernity. These haunt us when the routines fail, the narratives dissolve, and time disintegrates (p. 718). Then we arrive at the "crisis of time consciousness," which was staved off for a long while by residues of higher time (p. 719). But by the time we get to Baudelaire and Proust, that borrowed capital has disappeared.

And it is precisely our *un*happiness, our restlessness in these conditions, that, according to Taylor, gives "us cause to speak of a 'désir d'éternité' in human beings, a desire to gather together the scattered moments of meaning into some kind of whole" (p. 720). There seems to be something here that we just can't shake — that no amount of "rational" atheism seems to be able to excise. Might its persistence be reason to think that *there's something to this?*

b. Death

Another phenomenon that perhaps "tips" in this direction — tips, that is, toward an open *take* rather than a closed *spin* — is death, especially the death of our loved ones (p. 720). Here we seem to find another ineradicable desire for eternity that finds expression even in the secular funeral (p. 723).[51] Of course, this persisting desire for eternity "doesn't show that the faith perspective is correct. It just shows that the yearning for eternity is not the trivial and childish thing it is painted as" (p. 722). More strongly, perhaps entertaining the possibility that there is something *more* yields a better account of these phenomena. At the very least, unless one is dogmatically locked in secular spin, one should concede that "something important is lost when one forgets this. There is, after all, a kind of cross pressure here" (p. 722). Destabilizing immanentist spin should give folks permission to admit something that's been haunting them: "the sense that there is something more presses in" (p. 727).

In the final chapter of *A Secular Age*, Taylor considers those who *responded* to this transcendent pressure — converts. It is to their stories — and Taylor's account of them — that we finally turn.

---

51. Recall the scene we discussed above from Rieff's *Swimming in a Sea of Death.*

Conversions

To this point Taylor has offered an analysis of various "unbelieving positions" — the array of options that emerges from the supernova in our secular age. Close attention to these options begins to unveil certain chinks in the secure armor of closed takes (and certainly closed spins, which he sees as completely unsustainable for anyone with intellectual and existential honesty). In the final chapter Taylor moves to a consideration of "those who broke out of the immanent frame" (p. 728). However, I think he must mean those who "converted" from a closed to open *take,* since earlier (pp. 543ff.) he emphasized that we all inhabit the immanent frame: the issue isn't whether you inhabit the immanent frame, but *how.* In the final chapter of *A Secular Age,* Taylor invites us to consider exemplars who, having inhabited the immanent frame with a "closed" take, feel the cross-pressure of transcendence in such a way, and to such an extent, that they *convert:* to an "open" take, and usually to Christianity in particular. They don't thereby get a free pass out of the immanent frame, but they come to inhabit it differently.

The very strategy is worth noting. The goal isn't demonstration or proof; the point isn't to offer a syllogism that secures analytic truth. Instead, the appeal is to a "sense," a *feel* for things. For example, in the citation of a long testimony from Václav Havel, the operative terms are affective: "sensation," "I felt a sense . . . ," "I was somehow 'struck by love,' though I don't *know* precisely for whom or what" (p. 729). Taylor gravitates to those whose conversion was on the order of "sense." And the "story" of *A Secular Age* is intended to work in the same way, appealing to something like a "gut feeling," a "vibe."

This is why Colin Jager has described Taylor's method as "romantic" (and Taylor is happy to concede the point).[1] As Jager summarizes it, "one cannot simply extract the analytic content from the story; the story has to be told, experienced, undergone, in order for its force to be *felt*. So philosophic song is not something to be mined for what its content might tell us about the spirit of the age. Rather, philosophic song is a mode of critical thought because it forces its readers to undergo the very thing it is describing."[2] Throughout part 5 of the book, Taylor is trying to help us *feel* what it is like to inhabit the cross-pressured space of a secular age, and he has tried to empathize with "closed" takes, to feel what tips one in that direction. But now in the final chapter he wants to offer the immanentist a sense of just how and why some break out of the closed take. What does it feel like to inhabit this immanent frame differently, openly? That is Taylor's quarry in the closing chapter.

He does this by regularly pointing to *exemplars*. Would a Protestant proceed this way? Not likely. This celebration of exemplars bubbles up from a Catholic imaginary that accords an iconic role to the saints. Chapter 20 can be read as a sort of verbal stained glass constellation of Taylor's saints: Illich, Maritain, and Péguy.[3] So he's doing just what he calls for: "enlarg[ing] our palette of such points of contact with fullness" (*Secular Age,* p. 729).[4] The portraits *are* the apologetic.[5]

---

1. "Let me say to Colin Jager, I plead guilty as charged: I'm a hopeless German romantic of the 1790s" (Charles Taylor, afterword to *Varieties of Secularism in a Secular Age,* ed. Michael Warner, Jonathan VanAntwerpen, and Craig Calhoun [Cambridge: Harvard University Press, 2010], p. 320).

2. Colin Jager, "This Detail, This History: Charles Taylor's Romanticism," in *Varieties of Secularism in a Secular Age,* p. 191, emphasis added.

3. Compare the final chapter of Ross Douthat's *Bad Religion,* which celebrates Chesterton and Auden. *Bad Religion: How We Became a Nation of Heretics* (New York: Free Press, 2012).

4. Compare a similar role for stories about others in book 8 of Augustine's *Confessions,* the "conversion" book of Augustine's spiritual autobiography. For discussion, see James K. A. Smith, "Confessions of an Existentialist: Reading Augustine after Heidegger," *New Blackfriars* 82 (2001): 273-82 (part 1) and 335-47 (part 2).

5. Which is also why he privileges novelists and artists, whose mode of testimony is

The Temptation for Converts

In a way, Taylor suggests, all conversions to Christianity in our secular age are, to some extent, *reconversions,* conversions *back* to a social imaginary that animated Europe in the past. "The hold of the former Christendom on our imagination is immense, and in a sense, rightly so" (p. 734).[6] However, it is precisely this dynamic of *re*conversion that makes conversion fraught with a unique temptation: nostalgia. The convert sees the vapid flatness of modernity, and might also be lamenting the licentiousness of expressivist moralities of "authenticity," and thus casts an eye back to a very different understanding of our social order — a completely different social imaginary that was open to transcendence and articulated a telos for human flourishing (thus unafraid to articulate *norms* for human social life, etc.). Then you have a recipe for a kind of conservatism, or even a nostalgia, which emphasizes "that the deepest sources of European culture were in Christianity" while castigating the unfettered subjectivism of modernity (p. 733). This will be accompanied by "an unremitting hostility to liberalism, and to the 'idol' of democracy." This can lead to a kind of crusade for restoring the Holy Roman Empire (Action Française?), but at the very least it entails a commitment to "the idea that Christianity was essential for order itself." This whole package, Taylor concedes, is "very seductive" (p. 734). But he also thinks it is "very troubling."[7]

Taylor sees such nostalgia as perhaps itself a product of modernity, in this sense: in premodernity, there would have been a healthy sense of an expected "gap" between the ideals of the City of God and the realities of the earthly city (p. 735). However, the late medieval drive to Reform changed that. Reform changes our expectations, raising them, and thus

more oblique (*Secular Age,* p. 732). Once again, consider Douthat's point at the end of *Bad Religion* in which he cites Joseph Ratzinger (Pope Benedict XVI): "The only really effective apologia for Christianity comes down to two arguments, namely, the saints the Church has produced and the art which has grown in her womb" (p. 292).

6. This is Taylor at his most Hegelian: given our history, there's no way to "escape" it, even if we "overcome" it. Cp. Jürgen Habermas's way of emphasizing the continued role for Christian faith in Europe, given Europe's history. See Joseph Ratzinger and Jürgen Habermas, *The Dialectics of Secularization: On Reason and Religion* (San Francisco: Ignatius, 2007).

7. Though I don't see Taylor quite explaining *how,* unless he just assumes that we've already concluded that liberalism and democracy are good things.

also leading us to expect less and less of a "gap." Indeed, it breeds its own activism, a sort of realized eschatology. "This couldn't help but bring about a definition of the demands of Christian faith closer into line with what is attainable in this world, with what can be realized in history. The distance between the ultimate City of God and the properly Christian-conforming earthly city is reduced" (p. 735). You can then get a Protestant version of this, where Christianity is reduced to a moralism and becomes merely identified with the progress of "civilization" (p. 736), or a Catholic version of this, where the church imposes itself upon the social order as the instantiation of the kingdom arrived. What's problematic in both of these, according to Taylor, is a loss of the expectation of a gap (p. 737).

Indeed, later he'll note two ways of thinking about the gap. You can either think the gap is *incidental,* and that the problem is just with the present order, and thus is correctable if we could just get things aligned aright. *Or* you can see the gap as *essential,* short of the parousia, and thus be quite ambivalent about any hope of instantiating it in the present order (p. 744).[8] And converts, Taylor seems to suggest, are especially prone to the former (p. 745). Following Ivan Illich, Taylor sees the forgetting of this "gap" as its own kind of loss: "in identifying the Christian life with a life lived in conformity with the norms of our civilization, we lose sight of the future, greater transformation which Christian faith holds out" (p. 737). In other words, the moralistic closure of this gap (to which nostalgic converts are prone) amounts to an eschatological forgetting. This gives birth to forms of "corrupted" Christianity analyzed by Illich — of which Taylor also warns us (p. 741). So while he celebrates conversions, he prefaces this by a cautionary tale about the seductive power of nostalgia.

A Poetic Itinerary: Hopkins

Taylor is considering different "itineraries to the Faith" (p. 745), exemplars of different paths out of the closure of the immanent frame. His

---

8. Again, Fowler versus Pyle in Graham Greene's *Quiet American.*

most celebrated exemplar is Gerard Manley Hopkins, who reflects the post-Romantic way out through the arts, and in particular, poetry (p. 755).

This "way out" depends on developments in poetics in the 1790s, specifically the (Vico-ish) sense that language is generative, not just representative — that language does not just designate but also, in some sense, *makes.* "On this view, there is something performative about poetry; through creating symbols it establishes new meanings. Poetry is potentially world-making" (p. 756). But this also (re)introduces a kind of elasticity to language that creates just enough openness to potentially rupture the closed take on the immanent frame. This reenchantment of language is a direct protest against the flattening that resulted from univocity, which reduced language to designation (p. 758). But this can't just hinge on words in isolation, as if the issue were just finding the right lexicon, some "neologism" that all of a sudden breaks open the brass ceiling. Any "concentrated breakthrough in a word is only made possible through a host of others, references, invocations, questionings, against which background the performative power can act in this word." So "the power to make us resonate builds through a whole constellation, before erupting (as it may) in a single word or phrase" (p. 760).

In the new poetics, however, language is not just designative or a "pointer"; it is constitutive, a maker, a revealer. There are realities that are made manifest to us *only* in language, and especially poetic language. And it does so because it *resonates* with us (p. 758); it strikes a chord in us. But this is attended by a unique fragility: if poetic language reveals *by* resonance, then its revelatory power also sort of depends on us. What "resonates" can also cease to reverberate: "The language may go dead, flat, become routinized, a handy tool of reference, a commonplace, like a dead metaphor, just unthinkingly invoked" (p. 758). The same risk attends religious, liturgical language: the prayers "can become dead, routine" (p. 759). This fragility of poetic language's resonance calls for ever-new, "subtler" languages: "The very demand for authenticity — quintessentially modern — seems to drive us towards new languages, which *can* resonate within us" (p. 759). The worry that the language will go dead is a quintessentially modern worry.

Hopkins's project was to find a new, subtler language that would break through the ugly, sordid, instrumentalized flatness of so-called progress in newly industrialized Britain (p. 761). Insert pretty much any Hopkins poem here. If "dappled things" names something that reverberates for you on a crisp fall day, naming what had hitherto been only a vague "sense," an inkling — then you'll find Taylor's account (and Hopkins's testimony) suggestive. If not, there's not much more that Charles Taylor can offer you, because he doesn't think he can *prove* his point. But he'll keep pressing you: "Don't you *feel* it? Don't you have those moments of either foreboding or on-the-cusp elation where you can't shake the sense that there must be something *more?*"

Two Alternative Futures

So where do we go from here? Taylor finally succumbs to the temptation to make some predictions in light of all this analysis. If you're a "mainstream" theorist, you're still predicting a progressively less-religious future. But the problem is: the basement assumptions of this "mainstream theory" have been called into question, not least by Taylor's analysis. So if the "basement" of mainstream theory has been destabilized, then one has to at least entertain an alternative account: the structure of expectations built upon such a basement might not stand up.

This leaves room to offer an alternative account that doesn't just "explain away" transcendence, even if it still recognizes secularity₃. That alternative account is what Taylor has been trying to make room for all along. It is encapsulated on page 768:

> In our religious lives we are responding to a transcendent reality. We all have some sense of this, which emerges in our identifying and recognizing some mode of what I have called fullness, and seeking to attain it. Modes of fullness recognized by exclusive humanisms, and others that remain within the immanent frame, are therefore respondent to transcendent reality, but misrecognizing it. They are shutting out crucial features of it. So the structural characteristic of the religious (re)conversions that I described above, that one feels oneself to be breaking out of a narrower frame into a broader field, which makes sense of things in a different way, *corresponds to reality.* (emphasis added)

This is an unapologetic claim. It is not demonstrable except insofar as it offers a better account of our experience.[9] And the "better-ness" of that account is something that has to be *felt*.

But even if one might not *sense* the force of this alternative account, it might still be possible to imagine how the world looks for someone who does. If one builds on a different "basement," so to speak — if one begins from the assumption that Taylor has just articulated, namely, that there *is* a transcendent beyond that continues to press upon us in the immanent frame — *then* "what does the future look like?" (p. 769). Taylor hazards two interesting predictions:

1. "In societies where the general equilibrium point is firmly within immanence, where many people even have trouble understanding how a sane person could believe in God, the dominant secularization narrative, which tends to blame our religious past for many of the woes of our world, will become *less* plausible over time" (p. 770). This is in part because we'll see that "other societies are not following suit." However, there will be internal pressures as well, which leads to his second prediction.

2. "At the same time, this heavy concentration of the atmosphere of immanence will intensify a sense of living in a 'waste land' for subsequent generations, and many young people will begin again to explore beyond the boundaries" (p. 770). (The allusion to Eliot cannot be accidental.)[10]

9. This accords with what Taylor has previously called the "Best Account principle" (*Sources of the Self* [Cambridge: Harvard University Press, 1989], pp. 58-59).

10. I might append my own prediction to Taylor's crystal-ball report here:

3. Those evangelicals who have been raised and shaped by forms of Christianity that are roughly "fundamentalist" will either:

a. become taken with the modern moral order and thus sort of replay the excarnational development of modernity, just now a few centuries later, sort of catching up with the wider culture; so under the guise of the "emerging church" or "progressive" evangelicalism, we'll be set on a path to something like Protestant liberalism, a new deism; *or*

b. recognize the disenchantment and excarnation of evangelical Protestantism,

The aridity of that waste land, coupled with the persistent pressure of transcendence that cannot be explained away, will continue to generate "third ways" of various sorts. In that cross-pressured space, some will begin to feel — and be honest about — the paucity of a closed "take." And in ways that they never could have anticipated, some will begin to wonder if "renunciation" isn't the way to wholeness, and that freedom might be found in the gift of constraint, and that the strange rituals of Christian worship are the answer to their most human aspirations, as if, for their whole lives, they've been waiting for Saint Francis.

---

and also reject the Christianized subtraction stories of liberal Christianity, and feel the pull of more incarnational spiritualities, and thus move toward more "Catholic" expressions of faith — and these expressions of faith will actually exert more pull on those who have doubts about their "closed" take on the immanent frame.

Glossary

In *A Secular Age,* Taylor introduces a number of technical terms and phrases, or uses common terms in a special way. To help readers become familiar with these terms — and be able to recall their meaning easily — I here provide a brief glossary.

Age of Authenticity (AA)   Post-'60s age in which spirituality is de-institutionalized and is understood primarily as an expression of "what speaks to me." Reflective of *expressive individualism.*

Age of Mobilization (AM)   The political order is no longer divinely instituted; rather, it is *our* task to construct political order in conformity to God's law/design. Roughly 1800-1960.

Ancien régime (AR)   One of Taylor's "types" of religious identity, the ancient and medieval ordering tied religious identity to political identity: the king is divinely appointed.

Buffered self   In the modern social imaginary, the self is sort of insulated in an interior "mind," no longer vulnerable to the transcendent or the demonic. Contrast with the *porous self.*

Closed world structures (CWSs)   Aspects of our contemporary experience that "tip" the immanent frame toward a *closed* construal. See also *spin; take.*

Cross-pressure   The simultaneous pressure of various spiritual options; or the feeling of being caught between an echo of transcendence and the drive toward *immanentization.* Produces the *nova effect.*

Excarnation   The process by which religion (and Christianity in particular) is dis-embodied and de-ritualized, turned into a "belief system." Contra incarnational, sacramental spirituality.

Exclusive humanism   A worldview or social imaginary that is able to account for meaning and significance without any appeal to the divine or transcendence.

Expressive individualism   Emerging from the Romantic expressivism of the late eighteenth century, it is an understanding "that each one of us has his/her own way of realizing our humanity," and that we are called to live that out ("express" it) rather than conform to models imposed by others (especially institutions). See also *Age of Authenticity*.

Fragilization   In the face of different options, where people who lead "normal" lives do not share my faith (and perhaps believe something very different), my own faith commitment becomes fragile — put into question, dubitable.

Fullness   A term meant to capture the human impulsion to find significance, meaning, value — even if entirely within the immanent frame.

Immanent frame   A constructed social space that frames our lives entirely within a natural (rather than supernatural) order. It is the circumscribed space of the modern social imaginary that precludes transcendence. See also *immanentization*.

Immanentization   The process whereby meaning, significance, and "fullness" are sought within an enclosed, self-sufficient, naturalistic universe without any reference to transcendence. A kind of "enclosure."

Maximal demand   "How to define our highest spiritual or moral aspirations for human beings, while showing a path to the transformation involved which doesn't crush, mutilate or deny what is essential to our humanity" (pp. 639-640).

Modern moral order (MMO)   A new understanding of morality that focuses on the organization of society for mutual benefit rather than an obligation to "higher" or eternal norms. Thus the "moral" is bound up with (and perhaps reduced to) the "economic."

Nova effect   The explosion of different options ("third ways") for belief and meaning in a secular$_3$ age, produced by the concurrent *"cross-pressures"* of our history — as well as the concurrent pressure of *immanentization* and (at least echoes of) transcendence.

Porous self   In the ancient/medieval social imaginary, the self is open and vulnerable to the enchanted "outside" world — susceptible to grace, possession. Contrast with *buffered self.*

Reform   Taylor's umbrella term for a variety of late medieval and early modern movements that were trying to deal with the tension between the requirements of eternal life and the demands of domestic life. A response to "two-tiered" religion.

Secular$_1$ A more "classical" definition of the secular, as distinguished from the sacred — the earthly plane of domestic life. Priests tend the sacred; butchers, bakers, and candlestick makers carry out "secular" work.

Secular$_2$ A more "modern" definition of the secular as *a*religious — neutral, unbiased, "objective" — as in a "secular" public square.

Secular$_3$ Taylor's notion of the secular as an age of contested belief, where religious belief is no longer axiomatic. It's possible to imagine *not* believing in God. See also *exclusive humanism.*

Secularism   A doctrine associated with secular$_2$ that pushes for public institutions (schools, government, etc.) to be *a*religious. Roughly equivalent to the French doctrine of *laïcité* and often expressed in terms of the "separation of church and state."

Social imaginary Different from an intellectual system or framework, "broader and deeper than the intellectual schemes people may entertain when they *think* about social reality in a disengaged mode," a social imaginary is "the way ordinary people 'imagine' their social surroundings, and this is often not expressed in theoretical terms, it is carried in images, stories, legends, etc." (pp. 171-72).

Spin A construal of life within the *immanent frame* that does not recognize itself as a construal and thus has no room to grant plausibility to the alternative. Can be either "closed" (immanentist) or "open" (to transcendence). See also *take.*

Subtraction stories Accounts that explain "the secular" as merely the subtraction of religious belief, as if the secular is what's left over after we subtract superstition. In contrast, Taylor emphasizes that the secular is *produced,* not just distilled.

Take A construal of life within the *immanent frame* that is open to appreciating the viability of other takes. Can be either "closed" (immanentist) or "open" (to transcendence). See also *spin.*

Transformation perspective The view, essential to religion, that fullness requires the transformation of the human beyond mere this-worldly flourishing. So religion is not just a collection of beliefs about supernatural entities; it engenders a way of life that is transformative.

Unthought The (usually unstated) presuppositions that undergird an account of secularity and the decline of religious practice.

Name Index

Abraham, 119
Alighieri, Dante, 105
Amis, Martin, 61n.2
Aquinas, Thomas, 9
Arcade Fire, 67n.6, 69n.11
Arnold, Matthew, 101
Auden, W. H., 133
Augustine, 20n.34, 37, 69n.13,
  116n.31, 133n.4
Ayer, A. J., 8

Bach, Johann Sebastian, 75, 105
Bailey, Edward, 80n.3
Barnes, Julian, 4-9, 61n.2, 66, 75n.20,
  105n.17
Baudelaire, Charles, 74, 131
Beauvoir, Simone de, 68
Beckett, Samuel, 68
Begbie, Jeremy, 74n.19
Bell, Rob, 114, 115
Benjamin, Walter, ixn.1
Berger, Peter, 19n.31, 98n.8
Boersma, Hans, 50n.3, 114n.26
Boulton, Matthew Myer, 37n.7
Brooks, David, 124
Buckley, Michael, 53n.6
Burnet, Thomas, 72n.17

Casanova, José, 19n.32
Cash, Johnny, 88n.12
Calhoun, Craig, 19n.32, 55n.9, 61n.1,
  121n.39, 133n.1
Calvin, John, 32n.2, 37-39, 59
Camus, Albert, 3, 103, 127

Chabon, Michael, 78n.23
Chesterton, G. K., 133
Chua, Amy, 78n.23
Cioran, Emil, 68
Coelho, Paul, 89
Comte, Auguste, 13
Connolly, William, 21n.36

Dawkins, Richard, 2, 7
Day, Dorothy, xi
Dean, Kenda Creasy, 86n.10
Death Cab for Cutie, x, xii, 3
Dennett, Daniel, 7
Depeche Mode, 88n.12
Derrida, Jacques, 103, 127
Douthat, Ross, 85n.7, 89n.13, 133n.3,
  134n.5
Dreyfus, Hubert, 14n.18, 16n.26,
  17n.29, 22n.40, 56n.9, 73, 87n.11

Edwards, Jonathan, 115n.29, 116n.31
Elie, Paul, 10

Ferry, Luc, 122
Flaubert, Gustave, 5, 9
Fleet Foxes, 67n.6
Foote, Shelby, 12
Foster Wallace, David, x, 14-17, 61n.2,
  63, 86n.9, 130n.50
Foucault, Michel, ixn.1, 80
Francis, Saint, 81
Franzen, Jonathan, 11, 16n.26, 78n.22,
  102n.16, 124, 126n.45, 127n.46
Freud, Sigmund, 117

144

Subject Index

Action Française, 134
Agape-analogue, 56-57, 60
Agnosticism, 4, 6
Aladdin (film), 101n.11
Apologetics, 51-53, 96, 120, 133; *A Secular Age* as, 92, 105, 118, 120-21, 127
Art, 8, 9n.9, 41, 44n.14, 74-76, 104, 105n.17, 133n.5
Atheism, 6, 19, 26-28, 35, 59, 131; artificial-fertilizers-make-atheists argument, 81; new, 2, 4, 7, 9, 11, 17, 52n.5, 73, 96. *See also* Exclusive humanism
Authenticity, 84-85, 89-90, 134, 136

Bobos in Paradise (Brooks), 124
Buffered self, 30-31, 45, 52, 55, 64, 74. *See also* Porous self

Carnival, 32-33, 36, 40
Chartres, 105
Christendom, 12, 18, 19n.32, 22n.39, 31-32, 35, 37, 60, 134
Civility, 43
Civilization and Its Discontents (Freud), 117
Consumer culture, 68, 85-86, 89
Corrections, The (Franzen), 127n.46
Cross-pressure, x, 4, 8n.7, 14, 17, 24, 62-65, 75, 94, 96, 103-4, 114, 121, 123, 132-33, 139; creates nova effect, 73

Dead Christ (Holbein), 101n.12

Death of God, the, 100, 102n.14
Deism, 43, 51, 54n.7, 60, 73, 75, 116, 138n.9; providential, 50, 73
Disenchantment, 2, 3, 21, 28-29, 34, 38-40, 45, 55, 59, 61-70, 80, 90, 138n.9
Divine punishment, 114-15
Doubt, 3, 9-10, 14, 70n.14

Embodiment, 41, 58, 109, 113
Enlightenment, the, 21, 74, 76, 78, 110, 112n.24; counter-, 78, 111; humanism, 110, 117
Eschatology, 113, 135
Excarnation, 44, 58-59, 106, 138n.9
Exclusive humanism, viii, 22-23, 26-35, 38-41, 44, 47-48, 50-61, 65, 78, 100-102, 106, 122-23, 128, 137; challenges for, 110-13, 120. *See also* Atheism

Fragilization, x, 10, 62, 76, 97, 130
Freedom (Franzen), 78n.22, 102n.16, 124, 126n.45
Fullness, 12, 16n.26, 29n.1, 55-57, 62, 104-5, 108, 121, 122, 129, 133, 137
Fundamentalism, 4, 49, 73, 138n.9; modern, 72; secular, 7, 95

Garden State (film), 1, 102
God Is the Bigger Elvis (documentary), 97, 108n.22, 114n.27
Grace, 29, 32n.2, 37-39, 43, 57n.10, 119, 125, 127; eclipse of, 50, 55; nature and, 32n.2, 48

Idiot, The (Dostoyevsky), 101n.12

Immanent frame, the, viii, 4, 12, 26, 74, 92-99, 103, 110, 116n.31, 123, 132-33, 135, 136, 137-38

Immanentization, 48-50, 52, 56, 114, 122

Liberation, 78, 102

Lord of the Rings (films), 89

Lucifer, 107

Magic, 15-16, 39, 44, 89. *See also* Disenchantment

Methodists, 88

Modern moral order (MMO), 53-54, 65, 85, 87, 112, 122, 125-29

Monasteries, 32, 36

Music, 8-9, 14, 74-75; absolute, 75

Mutual display, 86, 126, 130n.49

Naturalism, 39, 92n.1, 99

Neo-Nietzscheans, 110-11, 119

Neo-Stoicism, 43

New atheism. *See* Atheism, new

Nominalism, 42-43

Nova effect, 14, 61-64, 69-75

Othello (Shakespeare), 101n.11

Paganism, 22n.40, 56

Pale King, The (Wallace), 130n.50

Pelagianism, 50, 55, 119n.37; cultural, 55, 60; epistemic, 50

Phenomenology, 18n.30, 69, 76, 99, 105

Plausibility conditions, 18, 22n.39, 60

Poetry, 63, 74, 118n.36, 135-37

Porous self, 29-30, 34. *See also* Buffered self

Problem of evil. *See* Theodicy

Providence, 48-53, 70; "new," 49

Reform, 33, 35-38, 44, 58n.13, 134; secular, 40

Reformation, the Protestant, 21n.35, 27, 35-40, 84, 106

Renaissance, the, 35, 41, 44n.14, 73-74

Romanticism, 24, 64, 73-74

Saeculum, 20n.34

Science, 2, 43, 72, 76-77, 81, 96, 100, 107n.21

Scientology, 108

Secularism, 2, 12, 21, 22n.39; minority view, 91

Secularization, 20-24, 56, 80-84, 91; of Christian notions, 56, 78; narrative, 138; theory, 20, 26, 28, 81, 83-84; thesis, 21-22, 79-84

Seinfeld, 126n.44

Self-consciousness, 14-15, 86

Sex, 114

Social imaginary, 24n.41, 26-29, 34, 45-46, 48, 51, 57, 70, 94, 134; of expressive individualism, 84-87

Sublime, the, 72n.17

Subtraction stories, 23-24, 26, 35, 40, 47, 74, 77, 96, 138n.9

Swimming in a Sea of Death (Rieff), 67-68, 131n.51

Taizé, 90

Theodicy, 52, 65-66

Thomism, 48n.1

Time-consciousness, 34

World Youth Day, 90

Worship, 16, 37, 43-44, 52, 59, 75, 139; eclipse of, 44, 52